Ecclesiastes

Life in a Fallen World

Ecclesiastes

Life in a Fallen World

Benjamin Shaw

THE BANNER OF TRUTH TRUST

THE BANNER OF TRUTH TRUST

Head Office
3 Murrayfield Road
Edinburgh
EH12 6EL
UK

North America Office
PO Box 621
Carlisle
PA 17013
USA

banneroftruth.org

First published 2019
© Benjamin Shaw 2019

*

ISBN
Print: 978 1 84871 868 5
Epub: 978 1 84871 869 2
Kindle: 978 1 84871 870 8

*

Typeset in 11/14 Galliard BT
at The Banner of Truth Trust, Edinburgh

Printed in the USA by
Versa Press Inc.,
East Peoria, IL.

Contents

Foreword

What is the message of Ecclesiastes? What, if anything, does it have to say to the church?

Many commentators approach the book as if it were an alien intrusion into the Old Testament, and useless for the New Testament believer. Others seem to hear different voices in the book, saying different things. The book thus preaches a mixed message.

First, this commentary takes the view that Ecclesiastes rightly belongs in the canon of Scripture, and as such is 'breathed out by God and profitable for teaching, for reproof, for correction, and for training in righteousness, that the man of God may be competent, equipped for every good work' (2 Tim. 3:16-17).

Second, this work assumes that the book has a clear message, not a mixed or muddled message. It takes seriously both the statement of the author himself in 12:9 that he carefully weighed many proverbs, and the comment by the apostle Paul that unless the instruments give distinct notes, no one will know what is being played (1 Cor. 14:7).

Third, this work assumes that Solomon, as the author of the work, was fully conversant with the recorded revelation available to him and that he would have made use of this material in his own reflections. In other words, this is a distinctly Israelite work, having its place in the larger context of Israelite revelatory literature. That is the book's proper context, not the context of the wisdom literature of Israel's unbelieving neighbours.

Finally, this work seeks to be a guide to the nonspecialist. Thus, there is little discussion of Hebrew grammar and vocabulary. The point is to focus on the message of the book. That message is most helpful in our day and may be summarized as follows: As one who believes in the God of the Bible, what may I expect from life in a fallen world, and how am I to live as a redeemed person in a fallen world?

BENJAMIN SHAW
Greenville Presbyterian Theological Seminary
Taylors, SC
January 2019

1. The Five Ws

Ecclesiastes 1:1-3

[1] The words of Qohelet, the son of David, king in Jerusalem. [2] Most vaporous, said Qohelet. Most vaporous, everything is vapour. [3] What profit does a man have in all his labour at which he labours under the sun?[1]

Who?

The five Ws (*who*, *what*, *when*, *where*, and *why*), the traditional journalist's questions, provide a clear way into the introduction for any biblical book. *Who* wrote it? *When* did they write it? *What* did they write? *Where* did they write it? *Why* did they write it? The answers to these questions provide the context for understanding the book itself, and provide the boundaries within which the book is to be interpreted.

With Ecclesiastes, the questions *who* and *when* are closely related. If Solomon wrote it, that fact also tells us when it was written—some time during the reign of Solomon. We will get back to a more detailed examination of *when* in a bit.

---

[1] My aim in this translation is similar to that of Alec Motyer in his *Isaiah by the Day: A New Devotional Translation* (Ross-Shire: Christian Focus Publications, 2011) where he says, 'My aim, rather, has been to bring you as near to the Hebrew as I can, as far as possible even following the Hebrew order of words' (p. 6).

For most of church history, the assumption was that Solomon wrote Ecclesiastes, along with the Song of Solomon, and most of the Book of Proverbs. However, in the nineteenth century, doubts about that attribution began to arise among some circles of biblical scholars. The denial of Solomonic authorship, however, was certified by the conservative German scholar Franz Delitzsch in the late nineteenth century, when he wrote, 'If Solomon wrote Ecclesiastes, there is no history of the Hebrew language.' His investigation of the language of the book had led him to the conclusion that the language was too late for Solomon to have written it. An illustration might help. Suppose someone found a play that purportedly was written by Shakespeare. But in investigating the play, the reader found such terms as 'cool' and 'neat' (both used in the way we commonly hear them today), terms such as 'astronaut,' 'beatnik,' and 'computer,' and phrases such as 'the cat's pyjamas.' These terms and phrases are clearly modern and thus much too late for Shakespeare to have written them.

Other scholars confirmed Delitzsch's conclusion, sealing the fate of Ecclesiastes. It could not have been written by Solomon. Thus, for more than a century students of the book have operated with the assumption that Solomon did not write the book, and that the language used in it reflects a time probably well after the return of the Jews from exile. Thus, the answer to *Who?* is a simple, 'We don't know.' Based on a late date, the conclusion has generally been that a Jew in Palestine during the post-exilic period, probably influenced by Hellenistic (Greek) thought, penned the book. Any attempt to connect the book with Solomon is usually ignored.

However, more recent investigations of the language of the book have served largely to overturn Delitzsch's conclusion.[1]

---

[1] See Daniel Fredericks, *Qoheleth's Language: Re-evaluating its Nature and Date* (Lewiston, NY: Edwin Mellen Press, 1988). His argument is summarized in his portion of Daniel C. Fredericks and Daniel J. Estes, *Ecclesiastes and the Song of Songs, Apollos Old Testament Commentary* (Downers Grove: IVP, 2010).

While the language of the book is still not typical of other biblical books from roughly the same time period (e.g. Joshua, Judges, the Books of Samuel), it should be remembered that Ecclesiastes is a very different sort of book. It is not historical narrative. Some of it is clearly poetry. Some of it is proverbial. All of it is philosophical. These three considerations alone should enable the reader to understand why the character of the language of the book differs from that of biblical books of a similar age.

It is my conclusion that Solomon did indeed write the book. My basis for that conclusion is, *first*, that the language argument for a late date cannot be sustained. *Second*, the opening verse identifies the author as 'the son of David, king in Jerusalem.' People who know Hebrew will be quick to observe that 'son' in Hebrew can mean more generally 'descendant.' While that is true, it is also the case that in the Old Testament, the phrase 'son of David' is never used to identify anyone but one of the immediate biological sons of David—Absalom, Amnon, Jerimoth (2 Chron. 11:18), and Solomon (1 Chron. 29:22). Solomon was the only one who reigned as king in Jerusalem. *Third*, the experiences listed in chapter 2 clearly have Solomon in mind. Even those who hold that Solomon did not write the book will concede that the author at least wants the reader to see Solomon in those experiences. *Fourth*, the Solomonic authorship is implicitly announced again in 1:12: 'I the Preacher have been king over Israel in Jerusalem.'

Unlike Proverbs and Song of Solomon, however, Ecclesiastes does not announce the name of Solomon, either in the opening verse or anywhere else in the book. This fact alone has confirmed to many that Solomon did not write the book. Our title to the book comes to us from the ancient Greek translation, the *Septuagint* (abbreviated LXX). The LXX uses the Greek word *Ecclesiastes* to translate the Hebrew word *Qohelet*. In classical Greek, *ecclesiastes* refers to a member of an assembly. The Hebrew word *qohelet* comes from a root meaning 'assembly.' It may refer to an office, hence a convener of the assembly, or perhaps a collector. The idea of 'convener' lies behind the common English translations of either 'Preacher' (probably also influenced by Luther's translation *Prediger*) or 'Teacher.' It appears that Solomon's purpose in not using his name in the opening of the book is because he does not want the reader to see this book as a kind of official pronouncement, such as a king might give. Instead, he wants the reader to see here, or rather to hear, the words of a wise man, unparalleled in both wisdom and experience. A similar situation might be found with a pastor who ordinarily is one who speaks with authority in the assembly of God's people. But there are times, outside that context, when he speaks merely as an individual, without the implied authority of his office. Solomon here takes the reader through his own reflections, aiding them in seeing not only his conclusions, but also how he arrived at them.

When?

Obviously, if Solomon wrote the book, it was written in the tenth century BC, sometime during his reign. But precisely when it was written during his reign is open to question. My sense is that it was written towards the end of his life. Some will object that by the end of his life Solomon had fallen into apostasy due to the influence of his wives, and that there is no evidence of repentance on his part. That is true, but that does not mean Solomon did not at some time repent of his sins. The Books of Kings present a compelling picture of the decline and fall of the Davidic monarchy, with even the reigns of David and Solomon subject to much evil. The Books of Chronicles, on the other hand, make it clear that the picture presented by the Books of Kings is not the full picture—otherwise the Books of Chronicles would not have been needed! As a counter-example, 2 Kings 21 does not tell us that Manasseh ever repented, giving us the impression that he died an apostate. But 2 Chronicles 33 makes it clear that, under the disciplinary hand of God, Manasseh did indeed repent, and spent the remainder of his reign trying to undo the evil he had done. Thus it is indeed possible that Solomon had a late repentance. Further, given the described experiences in Ecclesiastes 2, all of Solomon's building projects had to have been completed. This completion did not come until at least thirteen years into his reign (1 Kings 7:1, if the building of the temple and Solomon's palace are concurrent) and perhaps as late as twenty-four years (if the building of the temple and Solomon's house are consecutive). Given the other projects mentioned in Ecclesiastes 2, my guess is that it was even much later in his reign, as he began to appreciate the passing nature even of the great works that he had done, and as he had begun to learn, from sad experience, the dangers of unbelief and the toleration of idolatry.

In short, I would propose a date some time in the last decade of Solomon's reign, somewhere between 940 and 930 BC.

Where?

Those who hold that Solomon did not write the book usually argue that it was written by a Palestinian Jew. Thus, the place is the same as if Solomon wrote it, but the Palestine of the time of Solomon was a very different place from that of the post-exilic period. Palestine under Solomon was a united kingdom. It was young, with a sense of identity inherited from the reign of David in which the tribes were united. Palestine in the post-exilic period was old, tired, and far from unified. Jews inhabited the land but, much like today, there were various other peoples who inhabited the area too. The area of Judea was a small province in an enormous empire. At the time of the return from exile, that empire was under Persian control. The Persian was succeeded by the Greek Empire and its offshoots. Finally, not long before the New Testament era began, Judea became part of the Roman Empire.

It is in the context of a young united kingdom that Solomon offers this meditation. That kingdom faced no serious threats from other nations. It was a time of peace, rather than of war. In that context, one would expect a happy meditation; yet few, if any, would characterize the Book of Ecclesiastes as happy. It is sombre. Some might even say depressing.

What?

The opening verses of chapter 1 present a partial set of Solomon's main themes. Two other elements appear later. They will be introduced in due course. The primary theme is that of 'vanity.' The word occurs some thirty-eight times in the book, on average about every five verses. It is clearly an important idea, and one that must be properly understood. The question is, however, what does Solomon mean by that term? Vanity is not at a word that is in common use today, and the word seems to communicate not much of anything to the modern reader. Modern translations give a variety of renderings that probably are not that helpful. The NIV uses 'meaningless.' The *Common English Bible* and *God's Word to the Nations* render it as 'pointless.' The *Holman Christian Standard Bible* and the *New Jerusalem Bible* translate it as 'futile.' All of these versions give the book a negative beginning, and the reader then tends to approach the rest of the book in that light. But it is not clear to me that any of these translations faithfully convey Solomon's statement.

The Hebrew word that is translated by 'vanity,' 'emptiness,' 'meaninglessness,' and 'futility' is the word *hebel*. In literal terms, it refers to a *puff of breath*, a *puff of wind*, or *vapour*. Proverbs 21:6 says that 'The getting of pleasures by a lying tongue is a fleeting vapour,' or more literally a 'vapour driven away.' The word *hebel* is here translated by 'vapour.' In Ecclesiastes, Solomon is using the word figuratively. So what does *hebel* represent? It represents that which is passing, or insubstantial, fleeting. That which is passing can also disappoint or frustrate, so *hebel* can be used to refer to idols, which can never deliver on their promises, as in Jeremiah 10:3, 15.

In sum, *hebel* represents that which is passing or temporary. And that which is temporary is by definition insubstantial. It will not last. The sunrise may be beautiful, but it is *hebel*. It is passing. If you try to hang on to it you will inevitably lose it. Solomon begins his book by reminding his readers bluntly that this world is passing. Everything about it is passing. The person who tries to hang on to it will ultimately be frustrated and disappointed because it does not last.

The second theme introduced in 1:1-3 is that of 'gain' or 'profit.' It is a financial term, as the reader might suspect. Solomon faces his readers with a question: What profit (or gain) is there to a man in all his labour? It is an ultimate question. Solomon makes no attempt at this point to provide an answer. Instead he leaves the reader with the question hanging around in the back of his mind. Solomon will raise the question again in the book after he has had something more to say about the possibility of profit in this brief life.

The third theme Solomon introduces here is that of 'labour.' He does not have in mind merely the idea of work. The word has overtones of trouble and toil. Some scholars reject this idea, but the common use of the word elsewhere in the Old Testament has this negative overtone to it, and there is no reason to think that Solomon eliminates it in the numerous times he uses this term in the book.

The fourth theme that appears here is tied to the phrase 'under the sun.' As with the word 'vanity,' this phrase occurs close to forty times in Ecclesiastes. But what does it mean? It means the here and now, the life that we can access by our senses. It does not mean, as some seem to think, the world apart from God. Rather, it is just the world we experience every day. A couple of times Solomon uses the phrase 'under heaven,' but that is a variation and should not be taken to signify something else.

What does Solomon present for our consideration in these opening verses? He tells his readers that the world they inhabit, the world that makes up the universe of their experience, is a temporary, fleeting thing. To try to hang on to it is like trusting in idols. It disappoints and frustrates. Further, life in this world is laborious. Work is hard. There is an allusion here to the promise in Genesis 3:17 that 'By the sweat of your face you shall eat bread.' And overarching all is the persistent question, 'Is it worth it?' Is there any profit for a man in his labour?

Why?

What is Solomon trying to accomplish by this sobering meditation? Many interpreters, misunderstanding the significance of vanity, think that the message of the book is that life without God is meaningless, and that only when one turns to God in faith does life then have any meaning. Thus the book is essentially seen as an evangelistic tract, trying to convince the unbeliever to turn to God so that he might find meaning in life. Others think that Ecclesiastes is a less than orthodox book that teaches life is futile (a view distinctly at odds with the remainder of the Old Testament), and at some point a more orthodox writer got hold of it and decided to improve it by adding some more positive statements to its pages. This view also fails to understand the complexity of Solomon's investigations, as well as the subtlety of his understanding.

Instead, Solomon is leading the reader through a careful, and sometimes painful, examination of life under the sun. He wants the reader to see life in all its complexity, its difficulty, its evanescence, its disappointment, its frustration. The reader must not see the world through rose-tinted spectacles. He must not turn away from a careful consideration of the pains of life, and focus only upon its joys.

Human beings tend to take life under the sun both too seriously and not seriously enough. We take it too seriously when we fail to recognize and admit its brevity, its impermanence. We put too much stock in this world. On the other hand, we do not take it seriously enough when we ignore the ordinary events of life—the pleasure of a quiet evening spent with family, the small joys that occur from time to time in a marriage, the humour of a moment that is forgotten by the end of the day.

Solomon wants the reader to see this life truly and completely, with all its pain and pleasure. It is only when we see this life truly that we can make a proper evaluation of it and reach sound conclusions regarding it. So Solomon begins by announcing in no uncertain terms that this life is ephemeral. By this, he anticipates two statements that appear in the New Testament.

The first comes from James. In castigating those who presume upon the future, he writes, 'What is your life? For you are a mist that appears for a little time and then vanishes' (James 4:14). That is what we are—a mist, a vapour—and we had best not forget it.

The second comes from Paul, in Romans 8:20. There the apostle says, 'For the creature was made subject to vanity, not willingly, but by reason of him who hath subjected the same in hope.' The Greek word that the KJV here translates as 'vanity' is the same Greek word that the LXX uses to translate *hebel* in Ecclesiastes. More recent versions translate this as 'futility' or 'frustration.' I think 'futility' is entirely wrong, because God has a distinct purpose in subjecting the creation to *hebel*. 'Frustration' is better, because frustration is certainly part of our experience in this fallen world, but it presents only part of the picture.

The two passages taken together perhaps clarify Solomon's point in the opening verses of Ecclesiastes. This is a fallen world; but it is passing. We too are passing, and much more quickly than the world we inhabit. Because of that fact we need also to ask ourselves the question that Solomon poses in 1:3: 'What profit does a man have in all his labour at which he labours under the sun?' That question ought to sit in the back of our minds, occasionally calling our attention to it, like a tooth that sometimes aches.

Thus Solomon begins his meditation. It is not a happy beginning, and the picture Solomon paints will get uglier before it gets better. But this is the world we live in. We need to get used to it.

The organization of the book

The organisation of Ecclesiastes is an issue of perennial interest to commentators. Well over two dozen outlines have been proposed for the book, though none has gained general support.[1] The difficulty in outlining the book has been influenced not only by the general misunderstanding of its themes, but also by a failure to note its background. Though some have noted the influence of material from the early chapters of Genesis in the book, as far as I know, no one has really followed through on what that might have to say about the structure of the book.

In reflecting on the opening chapters of Genesis in relation to Ecclesiastes, it is striking that the order of the Ecclesiastes up to its midpoint (5:1-12) follows the events of Genesis 1–4. The second half of Ecclesiastes revisits some of that material, then in the next to last section reflects on Genesis 5. Thus I see the outline as follows:

1:1-11: Genesis 1—Creation

1:12–2:26: Genesis 3:6—The three aspects of temptation—wisdom, pleasure, and power

3:1-15: Genesis 3—the Fall

[1] David Dorsey, *The Literary Structure of the Old Testament* (Grand Rapids: Baker Books, 1999); Roland E. Murphy, *Ecclesiastes, Word Biblical Commentary* (Waco: Word, 1992); C. L. Seow, *Ecclesiastes, Anchor Bible* (New York: Doubleday, 1997); Craig G. Bartholomew, *Ecclesiastes, Baker Commentary on the Old Testament Wisdom and Psalms* (Grand Rapids: Baker Academic, 2009).

3:16–4:16: Genesis 4—Cain and Abel and the idea of oppression

5:1-12: Genesis 4:26—Then men began to call on the name of YHWH

5:13–6:12: Genesis 3:17-19—Toil as a result of the Fall

7–10: Genesis 3:6—The proper use of wisdom, power, and pleasure

11:1–12:8: Genesis 5—He lived, he had offspring, he died

12:9-14: The end of the matter (the lesson of the opening chapters of Genesis)

Christ in Ecclesiastes

There are a number of books and articles that intend to show the reader how to find Christ in Ecclesiastes. These books perhaps have their place, but to my mind they have a tendency to misunderstand the book itself. Thus, the reader will not find such advice here. It is not because I think Christ is not in the book, but rather that he is in the warp and woof of the book in such a way that in looking for Christ in Ecclesiastes the reader is apt to miss the wood for the trees. In what follows, I will occasionally draw the reader's attention to how Christ relates to what Solomon is saying. For the most part, however, I would remind the reader that Solomon is writing as a man in Israel at the beginning of the first millennium BC. He is writing to his countrymen, hence to the church of the Old Testament. He presumes his readers (or hearers) know the Law of Moses. They know the promise of a Redeemer. They themselves make up the chosen people (Exod. 19:5-6). In effect, Solomon speaks as Christ to the people of God of the Old Testament. So what we hear in the book is the voice of Christ. We do not need to scour the book looking for hints of Jesus, because his voice speaks in every word.

2. The Earth Abides, Men Do Not

Ecclesiastes 1:4–11

[4] A generation going and a generation coming, and the earth forever stands. [5] And the sun rises and the sun sets and to its place panting, there it rises. [6] Going to the south and circling to the north, circling, circling the wind goes. And upon its circuits the wind returns. [7] All the rivers going to the sea and the sea is not full. To the place where the rivers are going, there they return to go. [8] All words are wearisome; a man is not able to speak. The eye is not satisfied with seeing and the ear is not filled with hearing. [9] That which has been is that which will be. And that which has been done is that which will be done. And there is not anything new under the sun. [10] There is a matter of which one says, See this? It is new. Already it has been for past ages which were before it. [11] There is no remembrance of former things. And even of latter things which will be, there will not be of them a remembrance with those who will be afterwards.

Solomon now begins to press home his assertion that all is vanity. He does so by calling our attention first to nature, then to human experience.

In verse 4 Solomon ties human experience in with our observation of nature. Human life passes by. Generations come, and generations go. But the earth abides. The transitory character of human life is contrasted, seemingly, with the permanence of the earth, as if the human race were merely an adjunct to the earth. But there is more lurking here. Solomon is also reminding us of a promise made after the Flood. 'While the earth remains, seedtime and harvest, cold and heat, summer and winter, day and night, shall not cease' (Gen. 8:22). The earth remains. But it is not because the earth somehow is self-sustaining. Instead, God keeps the earth going. In the context of Genesis 8, the promise is that the earth, the stage on which the drama of redemption is played out, will remain until the final line of the last scene of the last act is uttered. Men are not permanent, for generations come and go, but neither is the earth. It remains as long as those generations of men cycle through to the appointed end of the drama.

Verses 5-7 focus on the natural order. Solomon emphasizes three things here. *First*, he sets out the repetitive character of the course of nature. The sun rises and it sets. Then it does it again, and again, and again, *ad infinitum*. The wind blows. It shifts its course from time to time, but it continues to blow. The rivers run to the sea. What Solomon envisions here is called the 'water cycle' by modern science. But as with the sun and the wind there is the continuous repetition of the activity.

The *second* thing Solomon emphasizes here is the sheer ordinariness of these things. At some level, they are the background noise to our lives. They are like the noise of a jet engine during flight, or the road noise of car travel. We notice them at first, but we soon become inured and no longer notice them at all. But they continue, according to the ordinary providence of God. They are the regular assurance that things are going according to plan, that is, God's plan not ours. Day and night, heat and cold, the regular course of the seasons do not stop, nor can we stop them.

The *third* point of emphasis here is the seemingly profitless busyness of these things. Solomon applies the question of verse 3 to our consideration of the ordinary course of nature. *Where is the profit in these things?* The sun rises and sets, only to rise again, as if nothing had been accomplished the first time around. The winds continue to blow, without any apparent accomplishment of purpose. The waters run to the sea, but the sea is never full. What has been accomplished? Where is the profit? The reader is left to ponder the significance of these things.

In verses 8-11, Solomon brings human experience to the reader's attention. All things are full of weariness. We reach the end of the workday worn out. Then we try to avoid thinking about the fact that we have to do it all over again the next day. We reach the end of the week, or the end of the year, and the same consideration faces us. As with the course of nature, there are three characteristics of this experience. It is repetitive; it is ordinary; and it is apparently profitless. 'Another day older and deeper in debt' as the old song 'Sixteen Tons' says. It is no wonder that the existentialist lists *ennui* (boredom) as one of the chief characteristics of life.

'The eye is not satisfied.' I grew up in the old days, when cameras and film were relatively expensive. My family did not take many pictures, but somehow we still ended up with large stacks of photographs. Today, people have thousands of pictures on their computers, and they still want more. People have thousands of songs on their mp3 players, and they still want more. We seem to have an innate dissatisfaction with what we have. In the next chapter, Solomon will point to his great works, but in the end they too do not satisfy.

'There is not anything new under the sun.' Solomon does not have in mind here such things as technological development. But even with that, what is a machine gun but a really sophisticated, and really effective, rock thrower? Instead, Solomon wants the reader to consider human nature. Throughout the millennia it has not changed or improved. Many theological liberals in the nineteenth century thought that the human race was moving toward the millennium, a golden age, the promise of a new day, when there would be evident a real improvement in the human race. Slavery had been abolished. Alcohol was being brought under control by the temperance movement. The industrial revolution was improving the lives of everyone. I am not saying those things were not happening. But I am saying that those things were being taken as evidence of the improvement of the human race. Then, at the beginning of the twentieth century, the First World War ('the war to end all wars'!) took place, and the liberal hope for the golden age was put on hold.

'There is no remembrance of former things.' When I was a student at Princeton Theological Seminary (1980–81), I worked in the library. Over the summer the library staff undertook a shelf inventory. This involved using the shelf catalogue (which had cards for all the books in call number order) and comparing that catalogue with what was actually on the shelf. Such a job can be boring, and we would occasionally pull books off the shelf just to peruse them. I remember looking at the book *Lex Mosaica*. It is a collection of essays on Moses and the Pentateuch, written by a number of scholars who were well known in their day. But that last due-date-stamp in the book was 1895. Or consider this lead paragraph from a story in the British newspaper *The Daily Telegraph* of February 4, 2008: 'A fifth of British teenagers believe Sir Winston Churchill was a fictional character, while many think Sherlock Holmes, King Arthur, and Eleanor Rigby were real, a survey shows.' Even those things, events, and people that we think are so important today will be largely forgotten fifty years from now, let alone three millennia from now.

These verses paint a grim picture of our reality. Repetition, ordinariness, apparent lack of profit or progress characterize not only nature, but human experience as well. The fact is, most people will make no apparent impact on the world. They will live, die, and be immediately forgotten by all but their closest friends and relatives. This isn't exactly the news we want to wake up to, but it is the cold reality that Solomon wants to ensure his readers do not forget. Solomon is not interested in sugar-coating life. Instead, he wants his readers to have clear understanding of the way things are so that they will have a real appreciation for his explanation of how things got that way, and how they might be fixed.

For the reader wondering about Christ in the book: this is the world Christ came to save. It is the world that he came to inhabit. For the sake of his people he submitted himself to this life—with its repetition, its ordinariness, its seeming failure to make any progress. So when this vision of life brings you frustration and disappointment, remember that Christ did not come to make you successful in this life, but to save you from its fallenness (and yours), and to bring you into a world where nothing is ordinary and where everything is new!

3. The Fruit of the Fruit

Ecclesiastes 1:12–2:11

¹² I, Qohelet, have been king over Israel in Jerusalem.
¹³ And I applied my heart to seek and to search out by
wisdom all that is done under heaven. It is an unhappy
business that God has given to the children of man to
be busy with. ¹⁴ I have seen all the works that are done
under the sun, and behold, everything was vapour and
shepherding the wind.

> ¹⁵ What is bent cannot be straightened
> and what is missing cannot be numbered.

¹⁶ I myself spoke with my heart saying, as for me,
behold, I have made great, and I have added wisdom
concerning all which was before me over Jerusalem. And
my heart saw much wisdom and knowledge. ¹⁷ And I
gave my heart to know wisdom and to know ignorance
and folly. I know that even this is shepherding wind.

> ¹⁸ For with much wisdom is much vexation,
> and increasing knowledge increases sorrow.

²:¹ I myself said in my heart, come now. Let me test
you with joy and consider good. And behold, even it is
vapour. ² With regard to laughter, I said, it is silliness.
And with regard to joy, what does this accomplish? ³ I
investigated in my heart, drawing along my flesh with

wine (with my heart guiding with wisdom) and seizing on folly, until I saw* that it is not good for the sons of man that they should act thus under the sun the number of the days of their lives. ⁴ I made great my works. I built for myself houses. I planted for myself vineyards. ⁵ I made for myself gardens and orchards. I planted in them all kinds of fruit trees. ⁶ I made for myself pools of water, to water from them a forest producing trees. ⁷ I acquired male servants and female servants and they became children in my house. Also there was the acquisition of cattle and many flocks for myself—more than all those who were before me in Jerusalem. ⁸ I collected for myself silver and gold and king's treasures and provinces. I made for myself princes and princesses and luxuries of the sons of man of all kinds.¹

⁹ I increased and I added more than all who were in Jerusalem before me, except that my wisdom stayed with me. ¹⁰ And all that my eyes asked, I did not withhold. I did not restrain my heart from any joy, for my heart rejoiced over all my labour and this became my portion from all my labour. ¹¹ And I myself looked back on all my works that my hands had done, and that labour at which I had laboured to do. And, behold, it was all vapour and a herding of wind. And there was no profit under the sun.

Solomon now begins his meditation on the navigation of this world. Underlying the section from 1:12–2:11 is the serpent's promise to Eve regarding the fruit, that it was 'good for food, and that it was a delight to the eyes, and that the tree was desired to make one wise' (Gen. 3:6). This same set of ideas appears in 1 John 2:16 as 'the lust of the flesh, and the lust of the eyes, and the pride of life' (KJV). 'Good for food' connects with 'the lust of the flesh.' 'Delight to the

---

¹ No one really knows what this final phrase means, and the diversity of translations reflects that.

eyes' corresponds to 'the lust of the eyes.' 'To make one wise' corresponds in part to 'the lust of the eyes' (in the sense of being aware of understanding) and in part to 'the pride of life,' which entails both wisdom and accomplishment. He begins with the last, the temptation of wisdom. Solomon was a man gifted with wisdom above all others, and he applies this wisdom to a study of wisdom itself, and its contrary, folly.

The supposition of the temptation is that wisdom will make life happy. But Solomon finds otherwise. His first conclusion is that *this life is an unhappy burden*. Man is busy, but unsatisfied, as demonstrated in the preceding section (Eccles. 1:4-11). Life is vain, and a 'shepherding [of] the wind' (1:14, 17). This latter phrase has been subjected to a number of different interpretations, and it is announced here as another major theme of the book. The phrase is made up of two words in Hebrew. The first is not a common word, and there is some debate over its source. The second word in the phrase can mean 'wind,' 'breath,' or 'spirit.'

Regarding the first word, it may come from a Hebrew root meaning 'to shepherd.' It may come from a root meaning 'friend or companion.' It may come from a root meaning 'desire or longing.' It may come from a root meaning 'bad or evil.' The KJV translated the phrase as 'vexation of spirit,' perhaps understanding the word to have come from the last suggested Hebrew root. Most modern versions translate it as 'striving after' or 'chasing after,' perhaps taking it in an extended sense from 'shepherding.' Robert Alter, in his annotated translation, goes with 'shepherding the wind.' Perhaps the modern phrase 'herding cats' captures the idea. All of these suggestions have some plausibility to them. All suggest something of the frustration of life, which Solomon then illustrates with the proverb in 1:15, 'What is bent cannot be straightened and what is missing cannot be numbered.' In other words, in this life, some things cannot be fixed. Yet wisdom seeks to fix all things. So wisdom is frustrated in that it cannot achieve its goal. In other words, the promise of the tempter is a false promise. Wisdom does not make life happy, and it does not solve all problems.

Solomon moves from the consideration of wisdom to the consideration of its opposite, folly and madness (1:17). This last phrase can be understood in a couple of different ways. Either the two items, madness and folly, are separate things, or they make up a hendiadys.[1] A hendiadys is a figure of speech in which two related terms are used together to express one idea. The English phrase 'law and order' is a hendiadys. So 'madness and folly' might be understood as 'the madness that is folly' or 'mad foolishness.' I do not think Solomon is considering insanity here. Rather, he is contrasting wisdom and folly. Wisdom is preferable to folly, because folly is madness, but wisdom itself ends up frustrating the wise man. Wisdom cannot deliver on its promises. Furthermore, as the proverb in 1:18 indicates, wisdom comes with its own disappointment. The wise man knows more than the fool does about the pain and sorrow of life. He is more aware of life's shortcomings. Think of Jesus mourning over Jerusalem (Luke 13:34-35). One wonders what the disciples were thinking when Jesus was lamenting. Jesus knew, in a way that the disciples did not, the sorrow that was coming on the city. Parents often mourn over their children in the same way. We see a child make a choice that we know will end up in pain for them, but they cannot see it. It is only the greater wisdom of the adult that enables him to see it. The child will learn only by painful experience.

Solomon devotes much of the Book of Proverbs to investigating wisdom and folly. Some of those results appear throughout Ecclesiastes. But he does not spend a great deal of time on it, having other matters to cover, and perhaps presumes that readers will be familiar with his other work.

From the consideration of wisdom Solomon moves in 2:1-3 to the consideration of pleasure, the lust of the flesh. In this

---

[1] Pronounced *hen-dye-a-dis*, with the accent on the second syllable.

investigation, as in the others in which he engages, Solomon remains objective. In other words, he does not devote himself to pleasure without reservation. Instead, he maintains, as it were, a mental objectivity, like the doctor examining the progress of his own disease. His conclusion is that not only does pleasure not satisfy, it does not profit. There is nothing to show for it at the end of the day. Those who devote themselves to pleasure find this out, but the deceitfulness of sin (and of the promise in the temptation) is such that the conclusion most pleasure-seekers draw is not that pleasure does not deliver, but that they simply have not indulged enough, that just a little bit more is sure to deliver the satisfaction craved.

In 2:4-11 Solomon moves on to the lust of the eyes and pride of life. He draws our attention to the idea of accomplishment and our own consideration of that accomplishment. In this Solomon, more than anyone else, had the opportunity both to accomplish and to evaluate. Others may have built more, but none were able to do so with the critical objectivity of Solomon. As a contrast, consider the case of Nebuchadnezzar in Daniel 4:30. While the boastful words were yet in his mouth, God struck him down. Solomon, on the other hand, catalogues his accomplishments, especially of the sort that men could see. His conclusion is that it was all vanity, all vexation of spirit. There was no profit in it. It is as if he could see down through the corridors of time and see that all he had built and had accomplished would eventually come to nothing. All those great buildings would eventually be torn down and disappear. All of it was temporary, and would vanish like the mist. Hence, accomplishment too was unable to deliver on its promises.

There is one particular note that should be made here. At the end of verse 8, the KJV says, 'musical instruments, and that of all sorts.' The ESV (along with many other modern versions) says, 'and many concubines.' The *New Jerusalem Bible* says, 'every human luxury, chest upon chest of it.' The *Common English Bible* says, 'every human luxury, treasure chests galore!'

The Septuagint says, 'male and female cupbearers.' What explains this diversity of translations? The answer is found in the annotation in the ESV: 'The meaning of the Hebrew word is uncertain.' The word occurs only here in the Hebrew Bible. The construction is a feminine singular noun followed by the feminine plural of the same noun (x and x's). It appears to be connected with 'the luxuries of the sons of men' which immediately precedes our phrase. So every translation is a guess. Whatever Solomon refers to here is connected to his accomplishments and acquisitions, but at this point, no one really knows what they are. The translations are no more than educated guesswork.

The only pleasure that Solomon found in all this labour and acquisition was the pleasure of the labour itself (2:10). That was his portion, his share. As for the results of his labour, it was vanity, passing, impermanent. The idea may be illustrated in sport. A player plays a great game, and enjoys that success, but the game ends and is soon forgotten. Another illustration may be found in handiwork. A craftsman may well enjoy the labour that he puts into producing a piece of work. But then the work is finished, and he moves on to another task. Or imagine a potter. He makes a pot, enjoying the work that goes into it. He is pleased with the result. He takes it out of the kiln and admires the piece. But something distracts or startles him. He drops the pot and it shatters on the floor. All the pleasure in the work is dissipated by the loss of the work itself. Thus Solomon's gloomy end in 2:11. Everything in time will shatter. Ultimately, all human accomplishment passes, and there is no profit under the sun.

In this last statement of 2:11 Solomon reminds the reader of the question raised in 1:3: *What profit is there under the sun, in this life?* There is no profit, nothing lasts. Everything under the sun, in this life, is vain. It is passing and temporary. That is the state of man, and it is something he cannot fix or change.

4. The Failure of Wisdom

Ecclesiastes 2:12-17

¹² And I myself looked back to reconsider wisdom and silliness and folly. For what can the man do who comes after the king? Only that which has already been done. ¹³ And I myself saw that there is profit in wisdom more than folly, as the profit of light is greater than darkness. ¹⁴ The wise man: his eyes are in his head, while the fool walks in darkness. Yet even I know that the fate of one falls upon all. ¹⁵ And I myself said in my heart, since the fate of the fool will fall upon me, then why am I so excessively wise? And I spoke in my heart that also this is vapour. ¹⁶ For there is no commemoration of the wise with the fool forever. Because already in the coming days all are forgotten. And surely the wise man dies along with the fool.

Qoheleth again considers wisdom and he does so in order that no one else will have to. After all, the person who comes along later will only come to the same conclusion that the author has already reached. This conclusion is that there is an advantage to wisdom over folly, as there is an advantage of light over darkness. The wise man is as the one who walks in the light. He can see where he is going. The fool is like the man who walks in the dark. He cannot see where he is going.

Yet the same fate meets them both. They both die. Wisdom protects the wise man in this life, while the fool meets all kinds of disaster, but the same end comes to them both. Wisdom, while having a practical utility for this life, cannot answer the ultimate questions. That is why philosophers are continually squabbling over the meaning of life. Human wisdom does not provide the answers.

This raises the question, 'Why be wise?' Neither the wise man nor the fool is remembered. This does not seem fair. 'And I hated life' (2:17) is the cry of the child who has just discovered that life is not fair. It is a true cry that adults have learned to stifle, and that is why *Qoheleth's* blunt statement of it makes us uncomfortable. Death, and the temporary and frail character of life, are evil. It is the man who recognizes this who is truly wise. The fool disregards this painful truth at his own expense.

5. The Curse on Labour

Ecclesiastes 2:18-23

[18] And I myself hated all my labour at which I had laboured under the sun because I will leave it to the man who will be after me. [19] And who knows whether the wise will come or the fool? And he will have power over all my labour at which I laboured and concerning which I was wise under the sun. Even this is vapour. [20] And my heart despaired concerning all the labour at which I had laboured under the sun. [21] For there is a man who labours with wisdom and with knowledge and with skill; and to a man who has not laboured in it he will give it as his portion. Also this is vapour and a great evil. [22] For what becomes to the man in all his labour and in the striving of his heart at which he is labouring under the sun? [23] For all his days are pain and vexation in his affliction. Even at night his heart does not lie down. Even this is vapour.

In Genesis 3:17-19, God pronounces a curse on Adam. It is not the curse of labour; that is, work itself is not a result of the Fall (see Gen. 2:15). Rather, it is that his labour will be cursed. It will be hard, and often unproductive, or minimally productive. That which would have been a blessing will now be attended with unpleasantness. Man will eat his bread by the sweat of his brow until he dies. This is the theme that Solomon visits in these verses.

At the end of a man's life, there is something left over. There is profit. Or at least it appears to be profit. Someone might say to Solomon, 'See, here is profit!' But Solomon makes the reader think beyond the obvious. He asks the question, 'Alright. There is profit. But what happens to it?' The seeming profit left at the end of our lives must be left to others. The vain thing about that is twofold. We do not know what they will do with it. And we have no control over what they do with it. What makes it worse is that we cannot change that. The reader who recognizes the frustration or vexation that this produces will not be surprised by Solomon's response of despair (2:20). This word 'despair' indicates the loss of hope. See for example, Jeremiah 2:25; 18:12; and Isaiah 57:10; where, in each case, the NASB translates the word as 'hopeless.'

We do not know what they will do with it. That is, they might be wise, or they might be foolish. They might make good use of what we leave them, or they might fritter it away.

It is possible that Solomon was thinking about his kingdom. He would have to leave that to his son, and he did not know what his son would do with it. He might well have suspected that Rehoboam would turn out to be a fool (which indeed he proved to be) and he lost most of the extensive kingdom that his father had left to him. I read recently that in many cases, when a man accrues vast wealth, it is gone from the family by the third generation. This is certainly not what the man who accrued the wealth would have wished. So that not only is the vanity of the situation the sheer frustration of losing control, but also the ephemerality of the profit itself. The profit soon dissipates.

The problem is exacerbated for the man who works wisely and well. A man pours his life into his work. Then he dies. Someone else enjoys the benefits of it. The man who does not recognize this is like the foolish man in the Lord's parable

(Luke 12:13-21). He had been successful, but he had not planned for his death. God's word to him is 'Fool! ... the things you have prepared, whose will they be?' That is precisely the issue that Solomon forces his readers to face. Work is hard. The results are uncertain. Even success is empty because death ends it all and removes from a man the power both to enjoy and to control. The man who makes this his concern finds no solution. It keeps him awake at night. The movie *Arbitrage* illustrates this. The main character (Richard Gere) gets himself into serious business trouble. All his machinations to fix the problem ultimately work (in the context of the movie), though at great personal cost. Had it been real life, he would still be facing the final arbitration brought by death. 'And ... it is appointed for man to die once, and after that comes judgment' (Heb. 9:27).

The first two chapters of Ecclesiastes are grim indeed. Solomon reminds men of their true state. They inhabit a world that God sustains and preserves, but the world passes them by as if they had no significance. Even other people take little notice of them. Furthermore, the promises of the serpent in the garden prove to be empty. The transgression did not bring the wisdom that was offered to Adam in the temptation, a wisdom that would bring understanding of all things. Instead it brought wisdom that was capable only of reminding man of his limitations. There were still things beyond his comprehension, and failings that he could see but could not fix. The pleasure offered in the temptation proved to be fleeting, ultimately unsatisfying. Even worldly success could not satisfy. It could be enjoyed, but only for a time. And the perceptive man, the wise man, understands that even great projects have their day. Then they too pass. All of man's life, all his successes, all his labours, are vain.

6. The First Respite

Ecclesiastes 2:24-26

[24] There is nothing good for a man except that he eat and drink and show himself good in his labour. Even this I myself saw that it is from the hand of God. [25] For who can eat or who can enjoy apart from him? [26] For to the man who is good before him he gives wisdom and knowledge and joy. And to the sinner he gives the affliction to gather and to collect and to give to the one who is good before God. Even this is vapour, and herding wind.

In light of this dismal outlook, what is man to do? Is he to reach Macbeth's conclusion?

> Tomorrow, and tomorrow, and tomorrow,
> Creeps in this petty pace from day to day,
> To the last syllable of recorded time;
> And all our yesterdays have lighted fools
> The way to dusty death. Out, out, brief candle!
> Life's but a walking shadow, a poor player
> That struts and frets his hour upon the stage
> And then is heard no more. It is a tale
> Told by an idiot, full of sound and fury
> Signifying nothing.[1]

[1] William Shakespeare, *Macbeth*, Act 5, Scene 5, Lines 17-26.

The reader would not be blamed for thinking so. But that is not Solomon's conclusion. He has positive advice for his reader. A man should 'eat and drink and show himself good in his labour' (2:24). The problem, however, is the question of how a man is to do this. How can a man recognize the hand of God's judgment on a fallen race as shown in the vanity of all aspects of a man's life and still eat, drink and be merry? In 1:13 Solomon said that it 'It is an evil business God has appointed to the sons of man to be preoccupied with.' That is the first mention of God in Ecclesiastes. This is the last of Solomon's main themes: *God*. All things are in God's hands and all things are ordered by him. God is inescapable. The vanity of life is the judgment of God on a rebellious race. But, here in his second mention of God, Solomon makes it clear that the hand of God is at work for blessing as well as for judgment.

There is a statement in this passage that requires some explanation. Verse 25 in the KJV says, 'For who can eat, or who else can hasten *hereunto*, more than I?' The NASB says, 'For who can eat and who can have enjoyment without Him?' Other modern versions have something similar to the NASB. So where does the KJV rendering come from? There are two aspects to the answer. The first has to do with whether the passage is speaking about enjoyment or hastening. In a technical sense both translations are correct. There is a Hebrew verb (*hush*) that means to hasten, and there is another Hebrew verb (*hush*) that means to enjoy. If that sounds confusing, think of the English words 'lead' (a verb meaning to direct) and 'lead' (a noun meaning a kind of metal). It is possible that in the early seventeenth century when the KJV was produced the translators were not aware of the second root meaning, to enjoy (which occurs perhaps only here). Or they may have thought that 'hasten' made more sense in the context.

As for the other difference—the difference between 'more than I' and 'without him'—is the difference between two Hebrew letters that are often mistaken one for the other. In this particular case, some Hebrew manuscripts read 'apart from/ without/more than I' while others read 'apart from/without/ more than him.' The *Targum* (an ancient Aramaic paraphrase) as well as the *Vulgate* (the old Latin translation) read 'more than I.' The LXX and the *Syriac* (another ancient version) read 'apart from him.' Thus it is not clear which is the original reading. If we take it as saying 'more than I,' the meaning is that Solomon is asking who, more than he, can enjoy things. He is in the greatest position to do so, being unencumbered by considerations of cost. If it says 'apart from him' the meaning is that apart from God there is no possibility of enjoyment. Enjoyment is a gift of God and is to be received as such.

Verse 26 also causes difficulty for many readers. The contrast appears to be drawn between the one who pleases God and the sinner, that is, a contrast between the righteous and the wicked. Thus, God gives the righteous wisdom and knowledge and joy, while to the sinner he gives the task of gathering things that will eventually be given to the righteous. As one commentator puts it, 'The good man's lot is awarded by him [God], as also the fate of the wicked person who accumulates wealth which he is not permitted to enjoy and ultimately passes into the possession of the virtuous.'[2] That is certainly a possible understanding, and perhaps the most common reading of the verse. However, it is contrary to human experience. There are many wicked who do not pass their wealth on to the righteous, and there are many godly persons who do not appear to have any more than an average measure of either wisdom, knowledge, or joy; and many who appear to have even a less than average amount of these things. If there is one thing Solomon is devoted to in this book, it is to making the reader face reality. Hence, the reader has to assume that whatever Solomon's statement here means, it accords with our experience of life under the sun. It appears to me that the verse

[2] Victor E. Reichert and A. Cohen, *The Five Megilloth, The Soncino Books of the Bible* (London: Soncino Press, 1952), p. 123.

is in fact saying this: 'To the person God sees fit to give them to, he gives wisdom, knowledge, and joy. To others, he gives the task of heaping up and gathering, work that is ultimately for the benefit of others.' In other words, who gets wisdom and who gets the hard work of saving up for others, is all in God's determination. It does not depend on righteousness or wickedness, but on God's decision.

Now some knowledgeable reader will object that the word 'sinner' is certainly used in this verse. That is true, but not particularly helpful, because the word *chote'* (sinner) does not necessarily mean sinner the way we hear it. It may mean simply 'the one who misses.' In this case the contrast is between the 'sinner' and 'the man who is good before him.' This does not mean a man who has proven himself righteous, but rather the man on whom God sets his eye. So the sinner in this case is the one who has missed, as it were, the eye of God. Ultimately, this verse lays out the mystery of election. God chooses one and not another. One gets wisdom, knowledge, and joy. Another does not, but ends up working for the benefit of others. This serves to emphasize that whatever enjoyment we may have in this life is the gift of God, and we are to enjoy it as such.

Solomon concludes that this, too, is vanity and vexation of spirit. That is, it is a temporary condition. It passes as soon as the people pass. But it also frustrates, or disappoints, because men have no control over these things. They are all in the hand of God. Furthermore, one cannot tell by observing gifts such as wisdom or knowledge whether a man is indeed right before God. Since God gives these gifts apart from consideration of the merit of the person, often those who are undeserving (in our eyes) receive much, while the deserving receive little. We cannot see to the heart of the matter, and the end is frustration and disappointment.

7. Turn, Turn, Turn, or Time and Eternity

Ecclesiastes 3:1-15

¹ For everything there is a season, and a time for every purpose under heaven.

> ² A time to give birth and a time to die. A time to plant and a time to uproot what has been planted.
> ³ A time to kill and a time to heal. A time to break down and a time to build.
> ⁴ A time to weep and a time to laugh. A time to mourn and a time to dance.
> ⁵ A time to throw away stones and a time to gather stones. A time to embrace and a time to distance oneself from embracing.
> ⁶ A time to seek and a time to blot out. A time to keep and a time to throw away.
> ⁷ A time to tear and a time to sew. A time to be silent and a time to speak.
> ⁸ A time to love and a time to hate. A time for war and a time for peace.

⁹ What is the profit to the maker in that at which he himself labours? ¹⁰ I have seen the afflicting task that God has given to the sons of man to afflict with it. ¹¹ All that he does is beautiful in its time. Also, eternity

he has set in their heart, except that the man cannot find out the work which God has done from the beginning to the end. [12] I know that there is nothing good for them except to rejoice and to do good in his life. [13] And also every man who eats and drinks and sees good in all his labour—it is the gift of God.

[14] I know that all God does, it shall be forever. Unto it there is nothing to add, and from it there is nothing to take away. And God has done that which they see from before him. [15] That which has been, it is already. And what is to be already has been. And God seeks the pursued.

This section is perhaps the best-known part of Ecclesiastes, due to the song written by the folk singer and political activist Pete Seeger in the late 1950s. The best-known recording of the song is probably that done by the Byrds in the 1960s, though the song has been recorded by dozens of singers. The arrangement of the material by Seeger made the song something of a peace anthem, though that has nothing to do with the passage in its setting here in Ecclesiastes. In 3:1-8 Solomon sets out fourteen pairs of events or times that characterize life. He sets the context for understanding these pairs in the first verse. Everything has its time. The phrase 'under heaven' is probably equivalent to 'under the sun.' That is, everything in this life has its time. Implicitly, however, these times are not set by man, but by God. That is perhaps the reason Solomon uses 'under heaven' here rather than 'under the sun.' Man is not in charge of these times.

Solomon begins with the most obvious pair of times: 'a time to be born and a time to die.' Though that is how most translations render the first part of verse 2, it is technically inaccurate. It should be 'a time to give birth and a time to die' (as it is translated in the NASB and the *Holman Christian Standard Bible*). It might seem a small point, but there is a subtle difference between the two. The more common translation seems to focus on the individual—his beginning and his end. The more accurate translation deals with the individual in the context of succeeding generations. A man does not just begin. A mother gives birth to him. He is by his very existence tied to the generations that precede him. It appears that Solomon may have Genesis 5 in view here. The record of succeeding generations of the human race at the beginning of time focuses on birth and death in a way that no other passage in the Bible does. A man does not choose his time to be born, nor, for the most part, does he choose his time to die. Birth and death come to a man unexpectedly, yet the times are fixed by the pleasure of God. The word in 3:1 that is usually translated 'purpose' also has the sense of 'pleasure.' It is sometimes used of the pleasure or purpose of the Lord, as in Isaiah 44:28 where it is declared that Cyrus will perform all of the Lord's pleasure or purpose. Solomon may be alluding to that sense here, where the times are certainly fixed by God.

The pairs in this passage are usually understood to function as examples of merismus. A merismus, or merism, is a figure of speech in which two contrasting terms are used to indicate completeness. Another way of thinking about this passage is to understand that Solomon, in speaking of 'a time to give birth and a time to die' (3:2), is referring to the totality of life. All times of a man's life are determined by God.

The next sentence (3:2b) deals with farming. No farmer can be successful if he does not know when to plant and when to harvest. But man does not create these times. They have been appointed by God. Man merely learns to recognize them. Solomon may again have Genesis 8:20-22 in mind here, with its mention of 'seedtime and harvest.' As with the preceding sentence, the terms form a merismus. So a farmer should not only know when to plant and when to reap, he should know the proper times that fall between those two, such as weeding, cultivating, pruning, and fertilizing.

'A time to kill and a time to heal' (3:3a). The reader should recognize that these times which are listed in Solomon's catalogue are not commands. That is, God is not saying that a man must kill at such and such an appointed time. Instead, Solomon is saying that when killing takes place, it is according to God's purpose. Likewise when healing takes place God's purpose is at work. This latter is a particularly important consideration in today's Western culture. We tend to think of healing as taking place at the command of the doctor, or by following a prescribed course of treatment. But it is God who gives wisdom to the doctor, and who makes the medicine effective for its prescribed purpose.

'A time to break down and a time to build' (3:3b). 'As with the fate of the individual, so it is with the house in which he dwells. If it is destroyed or collapses, or if it is built, that is not the effect of caprice but of design.'[1] In all these things, the chief consideration is the design or purpose of God. God brings times of weeping and laughter, dancing and mourning (3:4). We may have a particular purpose in mind, for example, purposing a time of joy. So a person buys a ticket to a football game. He expects that his team will win and that he will have an enjoyable time. But unexpectedly his team performs poorly, the other team plays well, and an expected time of rejoicing is turned to mourning. Or a couple sets off on their honeymoon, only to be involved in an automobile accident in which one of them dies. Such events come along, and all of them are in the hand of God.

It may well be that the reader at this point is a little uncomfortable with assigning all this purpose to God. It is probably because we tend to think we have a great deal of control over our lives. But the fact is, we do not. Yet there is nothing that is either out of the control of God or out of his purpose. This is a thought that should bring comfort to the

[1] Reichert and Cohen, *The Five Megilloth*, p. 124.

believer, and discomfort to the unbeliever. Our times are in God's hands.

'A time to throw away stones and a time to gather stones' (3:5a). Influenced by the second line of the verse, some interpreters over-interpret this line in an attempt to find something here that is not quite as mundane as gathering and collecting stones. That is, they understand 'casting away stones' and 'gathering stones' to be euphemistic. The words may be such, but I am not persuaded. In the ancient world, gathering and collecting stones had significance. For example, stones would be gathered out of a field in order to cultivate the field. Or they might be gathered for the purpose of building. They might be thrown away as unsuitable for a particular use. In any case, the line is a reference to generic aspects of life.

'A time to embrace' (3:5b). The idea that I always get when I read this line is a public display of affection. The line is not deep or profound; it is simply a truism. Part of life is learning the appropriate times and places for any particular action. All actions take place before the face of God; reminding ourselves of that truth can serve to hinder inappropriate behaviour.

'A time to seek and a time to blot out' (3:6a). This pair is something of a puzzle. While the first member of the pair certainly means 'seek,' the second means more to 'destroy' or 'scatter' rather than 'lose.' The closest similar use of the verb is in Jeremiah 23:1 where the Lord pronounces woe upon those who *destroy and scatter* his flock (NASB). The first verb there is our verb here in Ecclesiastes 3:6a. The second is a more commonly used verb for scatter. In Jeremiah 23:1, the two verbs are clearly intended to be synonymous. So what is the contrast in Ecclesiastes? Normally, we use the word 'lose' to indicate something unintentional: I've lost my keys. Here the word seems to have intent implied. So the contrast is between seeking (deliberately looking for) and losing (deliberately getting rid of). So if a man donates a coat to the Salvation Army he is losing the coat in the sense indicated here. This meaning of the pair is repeated by the second sentence of the verse, where the time to keep is more the idea of intentionally holding on to or guarding, rather than merely holding on to. We often hold on to clothing or other items not out of intentionality, but rather out of neglect. We forget that we have them. Here the idea is more like the man deciding to keep the coat rather than to give it away to the Salvation Army. The contrast is throwing away, again a deliberate action.

'A time to tear and a time to sew' (3:7a). 'Tearing' (or 'rending') here may refer to the act of tearing one's clothes in mourning, an action frequently recorded in the Scriptures. This is the meaning the *Targum* assigns to the reference.[2] Thus the sewing is the other end of that act. When the time of intense grief is gone, it is then time to pick up with life again, to mend the torn clothing and to move on. This does not deny the continuing presence of grief and loss, but rather recognizes that life continues, and the grieving person must continue in life, not shutting oneself off permanently in the manner of Miss Havisham.[3]

'A time to be silent and a time to speak' (3:7b). This is another example of the importance of exercising wisdom. There are many lines in Proverbs about the importance of discretion and carefulness in speech. This is a similar admonition.

'A time to love and a time to hate' (3:8a). Many seem to want to affirm that all times are times to love, and that no times are times to hate. The reader should remember that this is a merismus, and that the range of emotions is in view here. One ought, of course, at all times to love God. One also ought, at all times, to hate sin and its effects. There are times for joy and sorrow as well. Though we ordinarily do not think about them in this way, the emotional seasons of life come to us from the hand of God.

[2] Eccles. 3:7, *The Five Megilloth*, p. 125.
[3] A significant character in the Charles Dickens novel *Great Expectations* (London: Chapman and Hall, 1861).

'A time for war, and a time for peace' (3:8b). This is the point on which Pete Seeger focused, as if the end to military conflict were the supreme goal of life. It isn't. If war in the sense of military conflict is going on, it is surely to be desired that the conflict will end, as long as the resolution is a just one. But given that we live in a fallen world, war is inevitable, and no amount of wishful thinking or public demonstrations will bring war to an end.

Verse 9 seems to introduce a change in subject. Solomon here references 1:13. Since it is a difficult task that God has given to the sons of man to deal with, the question of profit suitably arises. The use of the phrase 'sons of man' is another hint for us that Solomon is meditating on the opening chapters of Genesis, because it might also be translated 'sons of Adam.' This phrase occurs seven times in Ecclesiastes, but rarely outside that book. Genesis 5 sets before us the genealogy from Adam through Seth down to Noah. In verse 3, we are told that Adam 'fathered a son in his own likeness, after his image' (ESV). This alludes to God's creating man in his image and likeness (Gen. 1:26-27). But Seth, and all who follow in his line, are after the image of Adam. That is, we bear the image and likeness of fallen man. Given that, it should be no surprise that the task God has given to man with which he is to be exercised is a difficult one, and one in which the profit margin is remarkably slim.

But even in spite of this difficulty, God has preserved beauty in the world. He has not condemned his fallen race to an ugly, joyless existence. However, things are beautiful in God's time. Our times are in the hands of God. The totality of our existence is carried out before his face. So the times of pain are balanced by the times of pleasure. The times of failure by those of success. The times of loss by those of gain. Furthermore, God has set eternity in the heart of man. The KJV translates 'eternity' here as 'world.' The word in the original does have that sense in later Hebrew, but it is doubtful that it holds that meaning here.

Instead, the idea is that God has placed us in time but with an implanted sense of eternity, the recognition that what we see under the sun is not all there is. But this also comes with frustration. Man is implanted with an awareness that there is more to life than what he can see, but he cannot figure it out. He knows that God has purposes and is working those purposes out, but man cannot comprehend that work. The Israelite who was familiar with the Pentateuch, as Solomon was, would have recognized that God has a purpose in everything he does. Such a person would also have recognized that God does give indications of the working out of his divine purpose. For example, the promise of a Redeemer is given in Genesis 3:15. But precisely who, where, or when that Redeemer will appear, God does not disclose. In the face of God's eternity and purpose, man is forced to see his own creaturely limitations. He knows but a little, and he sees but a little.

In light of man's limitations, the question rises, 'How shall we then live?' (to borrow a title from Francis Schaeffer). Solomon's answer is deceptively simple. The best thing that man can do is to enjoy and to do good in his life. The beginning of 3:12 literally says, 'I know that there is nothing good in them.' But, as with most interpreters, I take this as an ellipsis of 'nothing better for them.' The 'nothing better' sayings are relatively common in Ecclesiastes, particularly in this sort of context (see also 2:24; 3:22; 8:15). A man does not comprehend what preceded him, nor does he see what will follow. Man, as a creature, is tied to the moment. Thus, God's direction to him is that he be joyful and do good in the present moment that has been given to him. Solomon qualifies that direction with what follows in 3:13. He understands that even the ability to be joyful and to do good is 'the gift of God.' Later in the book he will mourn for those who do not have this gift. This is the answer, though perhaps not a very comforting one, to those who wonder why some people seem to be able to enjoy life, while others with the same, or perhaps even better, resources seem not to be able to achieve that enjoyment. When we talk about some having the gift to be able to enjoy life, we generally do not mean it literally. Solomon, on the other hand, does mean it literally, 'it is the gift of God.'

Verses 14 and 15 of chapter 3 further direct the reader's attention to what it means to admit that God is working his purposes out. Whatever God does is *eternal*. The same word is used here as in verse 11, where the KJV translates it 'world.' In verse, 14, however, the KJV translates it as 'forever.' The use of the same word, in the same context, within a couple of verses, generally indicates that the word means the same thing in both instances, something that the KJV translators failed to recognize. God's work is complete. It cannot be improved upon, nothing can be taken away from it. However much we might try, we are unable to overcome the work of God. This idea can be summed up in the title of the Broadway musical 'Your Arms Too Short to Box with God.' And notice how Solomon has ended verse 14. God has done it that men might fear before him. Many people do not take God seriously. Certainly that is true of professing atheists. It is also true of those who might say that they believe there is a God, but who have no time for, nor interest in, giving him a role in their lives. It is also true of those Christians who act as if God does not exist. All such are fools. When David said, 'The fool says in his heart, There is no God,' he is including the practical atheists as well as the theoretical ones.

Solomon's line of thought is this: There is a God. He accomplishes all his purposes perfectly and completely. We cannot comprehend those purposes, though God has given us a sense of eternity, hence of him and his purposes. We cannot overthrow nor improve upon those purposes. That should give us pause for thought. We deal with a being who is able to do all that he purposes, and who cannot be thwarted in accomplishing them. Such a being must be feared by puny and frail man.

Solomon concludes this section in a puzzling fashion. In 3:15, he alludes again to the conclusion of his opening statement (1:9). There is nothing new under the sun. What is already has been, and what will be already is. In the context, Solomon is reaffirming that God is working his purposes out. All these things have been, as it were, set in stone from the beginning. The concluding line of the verse, however, is not so clear: 'And God seeks the pursued.' This is a good example of a passage that is easy to translate but difficult to interpret. Most of the English translations appear to be attempts to explain the statement, rather than to simply translate it. Commentators also put forward a variety of explanations. The medieval Jewish commentator Rashi was of the opinion that it meant God pursued the persecutor, so that the evildoer has no profit from his crimes.[4] My own sense of the line is as follows. First, it must fit in with the context. This is not an extraneous line. There is no existing copy of the text that does not have it. Second, the order of the words in the sentence is important. Most commonly, the sentence order in Hebrew is verb-subject-object. In this verse, the subject precedes the verb, and it is linked to the previous sentence with the common Hebrew conjunction *vav*. So the sentence probably should be translated something like: 'As for God, he seeks that which is pursued,' or 'God seeks the pursued.'

What does the context have to say about God? That God has given men a difficult task. That he has made everything beautiful in its time, he has set eternity in the hearts of men, that God, as it were, hides from men the completeness of his work, that he gives man the ability to enjoy life. That nothing can be added to or subtracted from the work of God. That he has done all this that man might fear before him. What is and what will be has already been determined. In light of all that, the reader is led to this final statement in the section, the

---

[4] Reichert and Cohen, *The Five Megilloth*, p. 127.

meaning of which is that God continues to pursue his ends. He seeks that which is pursued, or that which is followed. That is, he is seeking to secure (a sense that the verb has) the things yet to come. Another way of putting it is, God is working his purposes out.

8. Corruption:
I've Got Friends in High Places

Ecclesiastes 3:16-22

[16] And yet I have seen under the sun in the place of
judgment, there is wickedness. And in the place of
righteousness, there is wickedness. [17] I said, I in my
heart, the righteous and the wicked God will judge. For
there is a time to every purpose and concerning every
work. [18] I said, I in my heart, with regard to the sons
of man for God's appraisal of them, that what is to the
beast is also to them. [19] For the fate of the sons of man
and the fate of the beast is one fate. As the one dies, so
dies the other. They all have one spirit. And there is no
advantage of man over the beast there, for all are vapour.
[20] All go to one place. All have come from the dust and
all return to the dust. [21] Who knows? The spirit of the
sons of man, does it go up above? And the spirit of the
beast, does it go down below the earth? [22] And I saw
that there is nothing better than that the man should
rejoice in his works, for that is his portion. For who can
bring him to see what will be after him?

Chapter 3 verse 15 brings one large section of the book to
an end. The next large section, beginning here, is a collection
of brief meditations on vain (that is, frustrating) aspects of life.

As a reminder, Solomon is forcing the reader to take a clear and extended view of the problems of life in a fallen world. He is requiring an unflinching look at reality.

The first of these problems is that of corruption. The introductory formula 'And yet I have seen under the sun' (3:16) indicates a new investigation or a look at another thing he sees about life in this world. In the place of justice and righteousness we see wickedness. Wickedness can be seen either as a crime against civil law or as a transgression of ethical boundaries. The context here is civil matters, whether secular (justice) or sacred (righteousness). A man may come to court looking for justice and find only corruption. The Lord's parable of the persistent widow gives a good example of this. It is also the case that law in the ancient world was much like law in the modern world. One gets as much justice as one can afford. Or in the sacred sphere, the sons of Eli are an infamous example. Being in charge of the sacrificial system, they extracted from the people whatever they desired. That fee, whatever it was, had to be paid before the priest would carry out the sacrifice.

In those situations, the ordinary citizen or worshipper would have had no recourse. They were forced by corrupt and unjust leaders, whether sacred or secular, into actions that went against what was right and just. The same situation continues in all nations today. There is corruption in the judicial system, and in the government bureaucracy that simply cannot be avoided. While the corruption in the USA may be less obvious than in other countries, it is nonetheless there. So where is there recourse? Recourse and retribution are in the hands of God (3:17). Solomon affirms here not only that God *can* judge, but that he *will* judge. All people are answerable to him, and will answer to him, whether they are prepared for it or not.

Verse 18 is very difficult. A literal translation is: 'I myself said in my heart, concerning the order of the sons of man [or concerning the matter of the sons of man, or on account of the sons of man] to sift [or purify] them God and to see what they a beast they are to them.' The sense is probably something like this: 'I reflected concerning the sons of man [again an allusion to Genesis 1-5] how God sifts them, in order that they might see that they are beasts to each other.' Even in a fallen world, where nature is 'red in tooth and claw' men ought to treat one another better than they do. Yet if one considers carefully the behaviour of men, they treat each other no better than the beasts. I do not think Solomon has in mind here the manner in which animals treat their own kind, but rather the manner in which they treat other animals. The lion shows no sympathy to the zebra. The fox shows no sympathy to the hare. The cat shows no sympathy to the mouse. Thus men treat one another. Solomon's point is not that men are merely beasts. He is not denying that man was created in the image of God. But he is saying that in the fall the nature of man was corrupted, and that corruption shows itself in the way men treat one another. It is an implicit critique of those who think that man is basically good. All of man's consistent behaviour points to the contrary.

Verse 19 highlights the one similarity that men and animals have. They both die. Animals die. People die. In this man has no pre-eminence over the animals. It appears that Solomon may be alluding here to the fact that it was man who ushered death into the world. All this death is man's fault. Furthermore, as with Genesis 5, every man's story is concluded by the statement, 'And he died.'

'All have come from the dust and all return to the dust' (3:20). This is an obvious allusion to Genesis 3. They all go to one place. This verse is often misunderstood. Some take it that Solomon is saying that men and animals go the same place: a shadowy *Sheol* from which none return. But we must be careful here. Solomon is not denying the afterlife. He is not denying the resurrection. He is speaking of life under the sun, namely what we can see. And what we can see is that all die. So from that perspective, man has no advantage over the animals. All is vanity. The lives of the animals are fleeting, as are the lives of men. All are dust, and to dust they return, as God affirmed in Genesis 3:19.

Solomon repeats the assertion in the form of a rhetorical question (3:21). 'Who knows?' Only God knows. As man surveys life under the sun, he cannot tell what happens to men or animals after they die. Does man's spirit, his life, go up above? Do the spirits of animals go down below? No one seeing events under the sun can tell. The answer is a matter of revelation, not observation.

As a side note, it would indeed be odd if Israelites did not believe in the ascension of man's soul after death. All of the surrounding cultures had a vigorous belief in the afterlife, and had very developed views of what took place after death. The Old Testament as a whole does affirm that man's life continues after death, and there is as well the affirmation of resurrection of the body. See, for example, Job 19:26; Daniel 12:2; Isaiah 26:19. But this doctrine is not developed in the Old Testament. It is left to the fuller revelation of the New Testament, with the resurrection of Christ as the foundation, to affirm the resurrection of the body. In this way, the Old Testament does not give in to the wild speculations of Israel's neighbours, but humbly relies on God to reveal the truth at the proper time.

Given that man cannot see what happens to him after death, Solomon again recommends enjoyment of his work in this life (3:22). That is his portion, his share. There are two senses in which Solomon's words here should be considered. First, that a man should do his work so that he can rejoice in it, so that he can, in the common use of the term, be proud of it. Whatever work he does, he should do it in such a fashion that he would not be ashamed. The second sense is that he ought to seek such work that he can enjoy and take pride in it. That requires that a man have an accurate knowledge of his abilities, so that he might choose a work for which he is suited, and which he is capable of doing well. As for this being his 'portion' or 'share,' it is what has been appointed for him, as, after the conquest of Canaan, the land was apportioned to the various tribes of Israel. In the division of this land, those in charge of the allotment were to see to it that each portion was appropriate for the tribe—smaller territories to smaller tribes, larger territories to larger tribes. Implicitly, a man is to think of his work as appointed to him by God. He is thus answerable to God for its performance.

Solomon ends this section with another rhetorical question, 'Who can show a man what will be after him?' The implied answer is that no one who can only see the present life can show him. Only God, who knows the future, can show him. And at this point in time God is not telling. He deliberately leaves it a mystery to man. Man must respond in trust and faith that God will indeed do what is right.

9. Oppression

Ecclesiastes 4:1-16

[1] And once again I saw all the oppressions that are done under the sun. And behold, tears of the oppressed and there is not for them a comforter. And from the hand of their oppressors, strength. And there was not for them a comforter. [2] And I praised the dead who were already dead more than the living who are yet living. [3] And better than both is the one who has not yet been, who has not seen the evil that is done under the sun.

[4] And once again I saw all the labour and the skill of the work, that it is the jealousy of a man regarding his neighbour. All this is vapour and herding wind.

[5] The fool folds his hands and eats his flesh.

[6] Better the fullness of a hand with calm than the fullness of two cupped hands with labour and herding of wind.

[7] I turned, and once again I saw vapour under the sun. [8] There is one and there is not a second. Also, he has neither son nor brother. And there is no end to all his labour. Also, his eyes are not satisfied with wealth. And for whom am I labouring and depriving my soul of good? Even this is vapour and it is an evil affliction.

[9] Better are two than one. There is for them good reward in their labour. [10] For if the one falls, his companion raises him. But woe to the one who falls and

there is not a second to raise him up. [11] Also, if the two of them lie down, they have heat. But as for one (alone), how can he get warm? [12] And if they overpower the one, the two will stand together with him. And a three-fold cord is not quickly snapped.

[13] Better is a youth poor and wise than an old and foolish king who no longer knows how to be warned. [14] For from the house of bondage he went out to become king, for even in his kingdom he was born poor. [15] I have seen all the living that walk about under the sun with the second youth who stood in his place. [16] There is no end to all the people, to all who were before them or afterwards. They did not rejoice in him. For this also is vapour and herding wind.

Solomon now considers the matter of oppression. Some of those who hold that Solomon did not write the book are of the opinion that he could not have authored this section in particular. After all, Solomon was king. He could have halted the oppression that was taking place in his country. How anyone with any experience of government could think such a thing is beyond my comprehension. Consider the following: man is fallen. That is the foundation on which Solomon's entire meditation is based. Given that man is fallen, he will work to his own advantage in whatever situation he finds himself. If he is in a position of power, his tendency will be to abuse that power. To quote Lord Acton, 'Power tends to corrupt, and absolute power corrupts absolutely. Great men are almost always bad men.' Even if the great men are good men, as in the case of Solomon, their own power is not so great as to be able to remove all corruption from their own government. Solomon was wise enough to see that. The man in power, if he is good, will try to minimize that corruption. Or he will try to set up a form of government that minimizes that corruption. But corruption in government is as impossible to erase as is corruption in the human heart.

Those who suffer under corruption have no comforter. There is nothing in the system of government—any government—that will, in the ordinary course of events, bring comfort to those who suffer at the hands of the corrupt. Admittedly, this is not good news. Many would like to see that changed. But given the ordinary man, and the ordinary state, the fact that there are the corrupt rulers and those who suffer at their hands is one of those things in life that even the wise man cannot change. 'That which is crooked cannot be made straight; and that which is lacking cannot be numbered' (1:15). Thus Solomon commends or congratulates the dead (4:2). They have moved beyond the sphere of corruption. Those who are alive still suffer under it. But better than either the living or the dead are those who have not yet been born, in that they have not yet seen the evil work done under the sun (4:3). They haven't seen the corruption, they haven't seen the sin. Here Solomon is not asserting that people have some sort of pre-existence. Instead, he is presenting a kind of hypothetical situation. Were there those who do not yet exist, they have the advantage over both the presently dead and the presently living.

From oppression (4:1-3), Solomon turns to look at work (4:4-6). He asserts that all labour and every skilful work comes from the jealousy of a man against his neighbour (4:4). This is probably a hyperbolic statement (something that features more than once in Ecclesiastes). Another way of putting it is that much of our labour and skill in work comes from competition. We see this to be the case not only in work, but in athletics, and in many other areas of life. A man wants to be better than his neighbour. But this also is vain. The advantage is fleeting. There is always another who is younger, faster, stronger, more skilled. We see this most clearly in sport. The old athlete loses his sharpness and his skills decline. Eventually he is replaced by another player. However, it also occurs in other aspects of life. The salesman loses his edge. He fails to keep up with developments. He loses the desire to keep ahead and falls back in the pack. Trying to hold on to the advantage is a losing game. Eventually, everyone loses.

Some may then conclude that there is no purpose in the competing. If one is ultimately going to lose, if one is ultimately going to be replaced, then why compete at all? Solomon's answer follows in verses 5 and 6. The man who drops out of the race, who ceases to compete, is a fool. His inactivity is to his own detriment. In the ancient world there was no safety net for those who refused to enter the race. They failed to compete only to their own loss. No one would look after the lazy man or provide for his needs. He, by his inaction, reduced himself to penury and want.

The solution to the conundrum is moderation. It is better to have one handful with quietness than two handfuls with an excess of labour (4:6). That is, a man should be satisfied with an adequate amount, rather than press constantly for more and more.

Verses 7 and 8 illustrate Solomon's point. A vanity, a foolishness that he sees in the area of work, is the man who is unsatisfied. The picture is of a man alone, an Ebenezer Scrooge. He has neither son nor brother. He has neither friends nor family, yet he keeps on working well beyond that which will meet his needs. There is not an end to all his labour. Yet his eyes are not satisfied with riches. How much is enough? Just a little more.

This idea was illustrated by a survey carried out many years ago in which two questions were asked. The first was, 'How much do you make?' The second was, 'How much would you need to make to be comfortable?' In all income groups, from the poorest to the richest, the answer was about twenty-five percent more. What they had would not satisfy. This answer among the poor is understandable. What they were making might not have been really adequate to provide basic necessities. Yet for the wealthy, what the poor might consider luxuries became necessities, and their eyes were not satisfied.

The problem here is that the man labouring for himself, labouring for far more than he needs, for so much that he really can't keep track of it, never stops to ask himself 'Why?' He deprives himself of good, rather than give up the pursuit of riches. Some translate the word 'good' here as 'pleasure.' It is perhaps not a bad translation, but Solomon's point is that there are good things in life that money cannot buy, and the insistent pursuit of money deprives a man of those good things.

The idea of a man without friend or family brings to Solomon's mind the whole idea of companionship. He investigates this idea in 4:9-12. Companionship is better than aloneness. Man was not made to be alone. Even before the fall, God said that it was not good that the man should be alone (Gen. 2:18). Thus, two working together benefit both more than one whose work benefits himself alone. Solomon illustrates with three earthy, practical examples. If someone alone falls, no one can help him up. If a man spends the night in the cold by himself, there is no one to help keep him warm. A man under attack can be overcome, but if he has help, the two are less likely to be defeated. As for the threefold cord, it is probably 'a proverbial saying quoted to round off the argument.'[1]

The man who thinks he can make it entirely on his own is a fool. Having others to help provides strength, protection, comfort, direction, guidance, and many other things. Whether we want to acknowledge it or not, we all depend on others for almost everything.

The connection between this and the following verses is unclear, as is the next section's connection to what follows. Further, there is some uncertainty as to the details of the situation described in verses 14 to 17. What is clear is the initial contrast between a poor and wise youth and an old and foolish king. Solomon here indulges in a number of twists on

---

[1] Reichert and Cohen, *The Five Megilloth*, p. 134.

standard wisdom themes. There is first the contrast between youth and age. Unlike our current culture, age in the ancient world was valued as being a source of wisdom. Rulers were generally considered to be more wise than their subjects. But here the tables are turned. It is the youth and the subject who are wise. It is the king and the old man who are foolish. In Solomon's estimation, it is better to be the young wise man, even though he is a subject, and, relative to the king, without resources. What makes the king's situation even worse is the fact that he can no longer even be warned. He will not listen to his counsellors.

The following verses almost immediately become confusing. 'For from the house of bondage he went out to become king, for even in his kingdom he was born poor.' Is this verse connected directly to verse 13? Who is the 'he' in these verses? Is it the poor wise youth? Is it the old and foolish king? It appears most likely that this is connected to the previous verse, and that the 'he' in question is the poor wise youth. This is due to the fact that, otherwise, there is no antecedent to the 'he.' Furthermore, it makes little sense for the old foolish king to be the one that is referred to. Thus the situation imagined is this: a poor wise youth in the kingdom of an old, foolish king. He has been in prison (though we probably must imagine something more like Joseph's imprisonment than our typical prisons today), but he comes forth and eventually becomes king, presumably on account of his wisdom. So a young wise king follows an old foolish king. Then in verse 15, there is mention of a second. Is this the same youth, as second to the old king? Or is this a different second youth? Again, it seems most likely to be the case that this is a different second youth. This second youth, with the support of the people then succeeds the first youth as king.

Admittedly, the passage is cryptic. But the point appears to be this: old kings are replaced; but especially when they are old and foolish, the people will prefer a young man. In this case, the young man's previous history is not a problem because of his wisdom. But eventually he too will be replaced. His wisdom ultimately will not keep him in his position beyond the time the people will tolerate. Though Solomon would not live to see this to be the case in the subsequent history of Israel, he had no doubt witnessed it in other kingdoms. Or if he had not, he could certainly surmise it. He was well enough aware of the fickleness of the people. The old foolish king would be forgotten. The poor wise youth would be forgotten. His successor would also be forgotten. Time would pass. This is the way of the world. All things are ephemeral and man cannot control them.

10. Fear God

Ecclesiastes 4:17–5:1-6[1]

4:17 Watch your foot when you go to the house of God and draw near to listen separate from the fools giving sacrifice. For they do not know they are doing evil.

5:1 Do not rush concerning your mouth and your heart—let it not be quick to bring forth a word before God. For God is in the heavens and you are on earth. Therefore let your words be few. 2 For the dream comes with a multitude of business, and the voice of a fool with a multitude of words. 3 When you vow a vow to God, do not delay to fulfil it. For there is no purpose in fools. What you vow, fulfil.

4 Better that you do not vow than that you vow and not fulfil. 5 Do not allow your mouth to cause your flesh to sin. And do not say before the messenger that it was a mistake. Why should God be angry concerning your voice and he ruin the work of your hands? 6 For in the multitude of dreams are vapours and many words. But fear God.

At this point in the book Solomon draws the reader's attention to that which is essential: the fear of God. It is a

---

[1] The first verse of Ecclesiastes 5 in our English Bible is 4:17 in the Hebrew text. In this chapter the verse numbers in the English version are supplied in brackets.

truism of Israelite wisdom that the fear of God is the beginning of wisdom. In spite of Solomon's seeming cynicism, which is actually realism, he does not deny this fundamental truth. Further, the reader needs to remember that here in Ecclesiastes, as well as in Proverbs, the fear of God is not fear as we think of it. It is not terror. It is not the 'I'm afraid of the dark' type of fear. Instead, it is the fear that arises when one realizes that it is the Creator of the heavens and earth with whom one is dealing. Genesis 22 provides a good illustration of what the Old Testament means by the fear of God. In that well-known chapter, Abraham, at God's direction, sets out to sacrifice Isaac. It is the ultimate challenge. Isaac is the son of promise. God has made that clear to Abraham. Yet God himself appears to cast doubt upon the fulfilment of his own promise. Nevertheless Abraham obeys. At the end, as Abraham raises the knife to sacrifice his son, he is stopped by the angel of the Lord. A ram is provided in the place of Isaac, and the fulfilment of the promise is assured. At that point God tells Abraham that he now knows that Abraham *fears* God. Abraham's fear of God is his faith that he will fulfil his promises. It is a faith that acts in obedience to God on the basis of the divine promises. A careful examination of the 'fear of God' passages in the Old Testament reveals that the 'fear of God' is the equivalent to 'faith' or 'belief' in the New Testament. That is why James uses Abraham as an example of faith, even though the words 'faith' or 'belief' occur nowhere in the account of the binding of Isaac. It is this *faith*, this *fear of God*, that is the focus of Solomon's reflection here.

Be careful in dealing with God. That sums up 4:17 (5:1). The man who goes to the house of God needs to be ready to hear. As often in the Old Testament, 'hearing' means more than just letting sound beat against one's ears. Instead, it is hearing with the intent of taking to heart what is said. 'It is better than' is implied by the use of the Hebrew particle *min* here. Solomon draws the contrast between the man who comes to the house of God to listen, and the man who comes to the house of God merely to offer sacrifice. While the law in the Old Testament clearly required men to offer sacrifices, the mere offering of sacrifice is insufficient. The prophets show this most clearly. In Isaiah 1, God declares that the sacrifices of the people sicken him. In Amos 5, God tells the people that he hates their sacrifices. The reason is that their sacrifices are the sacrifices of fools. They think that the mere offering of the sacrifice is sufficient, whereas God intends that they should come to listen, to learn, and to obey. The man who comes to hear is a wise man. A man who comes only to sacrifice is a fool. In his ignorance, he does evil, though he does not think so. Another way of putting it is that the man who comes to hear is a man of faith, a man who truly fears God. The man who comes only to sacrifice is a fool, a man without faith.

Connected with hearing and obedience is a carefulness in dealing with God. The man of faith thinks things through after hearing. The fool acts rashly and pays the consequences. 'For God is in the heavens and you are on earth,' says 5:1 (5:2). This is a summary reminder that God is in control, not man. God is the Creator, man the creature who is responsible to God. Therefore man is to be careful in his actions and speech. Solomon has not said much about the tongue to this point in the book, but he will come back and revisit the topic. Proverbs, on the other hand, has much to say about the tongue. Fools run off at the mouth. The wise man thinks before he speaks. His words are few but significant.

The following proverb in verse 2 (3) is somewhat cryptic, but the sense of it seems to be this: much business and the concerns connected with it bring dreams. The dreams considered here are not the meaningful dreams that we see elsewhere in Scripture, but rather the kind of dreams that disturb one's sleep and produce fear and frustration. As the dreams show the disturbance caused by much business, so the many words show the fool. This is a warning to the man of many words. Is the multitude of words a reflection of much wisdom? Perhaps, but more likely such a man speaks far more than he knows.

Verse 3 (4) provides further direction about our dealing with God. Consider well before you make a vow. A vow, at least in the Old Testament context, involved taking an obligation upon oneself for religious reasons. In the law, certain offerings were connected with the completion of vows. God expects vows to be kept. The worshipper is required to think through the vow before actually committing himself to it. The man who vows and who then does not follow through is a fool. He may be a very intelligent man. He may be a very rich or successful man, but he is nonetheless a fool. God will hold him accountable for his broken vow.

There is some difference between the way vows were considered in the Old Testament and the way they are considered today. In the Old Testament, vows are mentioned primarily in the Pentateuch, infrequently in Psalms, and rarely elsewhere. Thus the vow seems to refer to an occasional or special consecration of oneself to God. As such, the vow would not have been merely a private statement made to oneself, but a public statement made before witnesses, perhaps even at the temple before a priest. It does not appear to include many things that today would be called vows, such as wedding vows or membership vows. The thing vowed was not something ordinarily required. Since it was a serious, extraordinary commitment, a vow was not something that should have been undertaken rashly or without careful forethought and planning.

Since a vow was not required, Solomon makes the point in verse 4 (5) that if a man does not intend to fulfil the vow, he is better off not making it in the first place. The idea here is a little bit like volunteering in the military. Veterans will generally tell you that if an officer asks for volunteers, then it is usually for an undertaking no one really wants to do! Further, if the man does make a vow, he better go ahead and fulfil it. The only exception (and this is not in Solomon's purview) would be a wicked vow, such as Jephthah's. A wicked vow is a sin to be repented of, not fulfilled.

Verse 5 (6) is a further caution against foolish vows. Don't let your mouth get you into trouble. Again, there is the implicit warning against rash and careless speaking. There is some debate about who the 'messenger' is. Some commentators take it to be a temple official whose duty it is to follow up on vows, to make sure they had been fulfilled. Others take it to refer to a special angelic messenger, though the former fits the context better: that is, a man who made a vow that he later regretted, who might well be tempted to tell the temple messenger that it had been a genuine mistake. In that case, he would only be multiplying his problems. The witnesses before whom he made the vow would be called in, and he would be called to account. He would eventually have to pay off the vow. In sum, Solomon's advice is that when one deals with God, one does so seriously and with forethought. God takes these things seriously. We ought to also.

Verse 6 (7) is connected with verse 2(3) and probably makes essentially the same point. Much business with all of its concerns, a focus on money, and carelessness in speaking, all these things combine to put oneself in trouble with God. Instead, one should fear God. That is, one should walk by faith. A vow is an act of faith. Failure to fulfil it is an act of faithlessness.

11. The Problem of Stuff

Ecclesiastes 5:7-17

⁷ If the oppressing of the poor and the stalling of judgment and righteousness you see in the province, do not be surprised concerning the situation. For a high one above the high one watches, and higher ones over them. ⁸ And the profit of land in the whole of it: a king is served by the fields. ⁹ One who loves money is not satisfied with money. And who is the one loving wealth will not be satisfied with income. Also, this is vapour.

¹⁰ When goods multiply, those who eat it multiply. Then what is the benefit to its master but what his eyes see? ¹¹ Sweet is the sleep of the one serving, whether little or much he eats. But there is no satiety to the rich. There is no resting for him in sleep. ¹² There is a painful evil I have seen under the sun: riches kept by their master to his hurt.

¹³ And those riches perish in an evil business. And he begets a son and there is nothing in his hand. ¹⁴ Just as he went out from the belly of his mother naked, he shall return to go just as he came. And he shall carry nothing in his labour that goes in his hand. ¹⁵ And also this is a painful evil—everything just as he came, so shall he go. And what is the profit to him? That he labours for vapour. ¹⁶ Even all his days he ate in darkness, and greatly vexed in his suffering and discontent. ¹⁷ Behold what I

> myself have seen is good: what is beautiful is to eat and
> to drink and to see good in all his labour at which he
> labours under the sun the numbers of the days of his life
> which God gives him. For that is his portion.

This section deals primarily with matters of wealth and poverty, though the 'flow' of the argument might not be entirely clear. Verse 7 (8) has provoked a fair amount of discussion among the commentators. The first half of the verse is unremarkable. 'If the oppressing of the poor and the stalling of judgment and righteousness you see in the province, do not be surprised concerning the situation.' Solomon has earlier commented on the ordinariness of oppression, and the inability of even the wisest king to eradicate it from his kingdom. So here he tells the reader not to be shocked or surprised by it. Today, especially in the West, people seem to be surprised, even shocked, when they run into examples of oppression, or of criminal behaviour by representatives of the state. Most people in the West operate with the belief that people are basically good. As a result, such corruption surprises them. Solomon has a realistic view of human nature. He recommends that we should share that view. Corruption should not surprise us. Solomon does not mean for us to infer from this that we ought not to take steps to punish corrupt and abusive officials. He is not advocating complacency in the face of evil. But he does want his readers to be realistic. In a vain world, you will never get rid of all corruption.

The second part of the verse is a more difficult matter. 'For a high one above the high one watches, and higher ones over them.' This has been taken in either a positive or a negative sense. The negative view is reflected in the NLT translation: 'For every official is under orders from higher up, and matters of justice get lost in red tape and bureaucracy.' The idea is that the high one is a bureaucratic official, being watched by another, with still others above them. With all the levels of bureaucracy, judgment and righteousness get lost in the shuffle. A similar interpretation appears in the *Christian Standard Bible*.

However, another interpretation is possible. Some commentators take the view that the idea of higher and higher officials introduces a level of accountability by the higher officials. Hence, corruption at the lower levels will be corrected by oversight. We had a good example of that with an Internal Revenue Service (IRS) scandal in the US. The problem was really a handful of low-level bureaucrats in Cincinnati, and as soon as the upper echelons heard about it, they set out to fix the problem. The previous two sentences were tongue-in-cheek.[1] It strikes me as an interpretation out of accord with Solomon's view of human nature. Though I don't care for the NLT as a translation, as a commentary on this verse I think it is to the point.

It is possible, however, to take another interpretation that is positive. That is the view that the plural 'higher ones' at the end of the verse should perhaps be taken as a superlative; that is, 'there is a highest one over all of them.' In this view, God is the highest one, and he is the one who will bring all these corrupt officials to justice. Admittedly, that is not much encouragement in the short term, but it does assure us that in the longer term all things will be sorted out.

Of all these views, my own sense is that it is most likely the case that the passage is directing the reader to consider that corruption is endemic to human bureaucracies, no matter what level of bureaucracy is under consideration. There may be an implied encouragement to believe that God will sort everything out in the end, but it is not explicit.

Verse 8 (9) is another point of contention. A literal rendering is, 'And profit of a land in all of it, a king to a field is served.' Of this verse, one commentator says, 'An obscure and

---

[1] For those interested, the full report on the U.S. House Committee on Oversight and Government Reform can be found here: https://oversight. house.gov/wp-content/uploads/2014/12/December-2014-IRS-Report.pdf.

difficult verse which has been variously explained.'[2] There are several problems with the interpretation of this verse. 'King' is mentioned only seven times in the entire book, and two of those references are to the author himself. There is no other mention of 'king' in the immediate context, so the connection of this verse either with what precedes or with what follows is tenuous. Second, what does it mean that the king is served by the field? The word 'field' here is different from the word 'land' in the first part of the verse. 'Field' (*sadeh*) most commonly refers to cultivable land, as opposed to 'wilderness' (*midbar*), though it may refer only to open land, whether cultivable or not. 'Land' in the first part of the verse generally refers to 'territory,' such as in the phrase 'the land of Israel.'

The first part of the verse is capable of more than one translation, but virtually all the English versions are more like a paraphrase that attempts to explain the verse rather than simply render the Hebrew into English. The questions that arise from the Hebrew text are: 1. What is meant by 'the profit of a land'? 2. What does the 'in all' mean? There are different possibilities, such as in everything, in the whole, on all accounts. 3. What is the antecedent of the 'it'? In the second part of the verse, one may question what is meant by a king being served by a field?

My suggestion for this verse is, first, that is it not directly linked to either what follows or to what precedes, though most translations put it in the same paragraph as verses 6-7 (7-8), implying that it somehow goes with them. There is nothing in verse 8 (9) that clearly connects it to the issue of bureaucratic corruption in the two preceding verses. Further, there is no connection with what follows. So this is perhaps a proverbial statement that suffers from the difficulty of many biblical proverbs: they are hard to interpret, because they have almost no context.

Second, I take the two halves of the verse to be separate

[2] Reichert and Cohen, *The Five Megilloth*, p. 141.

statements. They are related in the way that two halves of a proverb are related, but they do not properly mix. This is different from what a number of English versions do, such as the CEB, which also manages to eliminate the king: 'But the land's yield should be for everyone if the field is cultivated.'

Third, I take the first half of the verse as a noun clause. That is, a form of the verb 'to be' is implied in the construction.

Fourth, the verse does have to do with the larger context, which deals with stuff.

With all that in view, I would translate the verse this way: 'And the profit of land in the whole of it: a king is served by the fields.' The meaning is that a land (or a territory) delivers profit from the whole of it, not just from a part, and that the king is served by the profit from the land. I take 'field' in the second part of the verse to be a poetic parallel for 'land' in the first half of the verse, and thus to have essentially the same meaning.

The idea of the verse could well be summarised as follows: 'Agriculture comes first among human activities. Without it there would be no merchants, no courtiers, no kings, no poets and no philosophers. The only true form of wealth is that produced by the soil.'[3]

Solomon's reflection on stuff continues in verse 9-10 (10-11). He makes the shrewd observation that people who love stuff are ultimately not satisfied with stuff. 'Just a little more' is always their answer to the question 'How much?' This too is vain; that is, it is characteristic of life in a fallen world.

In the next verse, Solomon also observes that person who has more stuff will have more hangers-on. In the end, his only real advantage is that he gets to see more goods, but he also gets to watch them leave. The man with a small piece of land and only his own family to provide for may indeed make himself quite comfortable. The man with so much land that he requires workers to take care of it, must provide for

[3] John Eliot Gardiner, *Bach: Music in the Castle of Heaven* (New York: Vintage Books, 2013), p. 23.

those workers as well as for himself. Further, there are societal expectations regarding his general largesse. So while he has more, he spends more, and may in the end be less satisfied than the man who has only a little. This is the point that Solomon makes in verse 11 (12). A man who has little has little to worry about. A man who has much is always worried about what he has, both in the sense of wanting to keep it safe, and in wanting to increase it. These observations are proverbial in nature, so not true in every case. But they are so generally true that Solomon desires the reader to pay careful attention to them, and ask himself the wise questions that would spring from them. The primary question, of course, is: Do I really want to be tied down by stuff?

The last episode in this section also deals with a man who has too much, at least to start with. This is more complicated than might appear at first glance. The grievous evil that Solomon has seen is, first of all, riches kept by their owner to his own hurt. The author does not expand on the statement, so let us puzzle it out. Solomon is probably building on the comments of the preceding episode; that is, a man who has so much wealth that it becomes a burden to him. Why is that a grievous evil? Because, in seeming to have gained profit, the man has not profited. He has not, ultimately, benefitted from his amassed wealth. Solomon doesn't tell us what the man should do. He simply warns us of the fact that this is the kind of thing that happens in a fallen world.

Verse 13 (14) piggybacks on verse 12 (13) but is, in my mind, a separate episode, or a separate consideration. In this case, the man does not retain his money. Instead he loses it in a bad business venture. Perhaps he has engaged in trade, and the cargo he invested in has been lost. This was not an uncommon event in ancient times, when caravans were subject to robbers, or corrupt caravan masters. The latter might sell the goods for his own profit, then tell the shipper that he had been robbed. On sea, cargo was liable to be lost due to storms and shipwrecks as well as to piracy. In any case, this man has lost his wealth.

If he has a son, he has nothing to leave to him. A man who was unable to provide for his family would have been deeply shamed in that culture. He is left at the end in the same condition in which he entered the world—without possessions or resources. He comes to the end of his life with nothing, with no profit. So Solomon again asks the question, where is the profit in this life under the sun? All this man laboured for is gone. He might as well have been labouring for the wind. The end of his life is described in verse 16 (17): much vexation, sickness, and wrath. There is only darkness and disappointment.

I once had a professor who was something of a notorious drinker, though he was friendly and popular with students. In talking about him one day, another student related the story that this professor had been working on a particular book for years. He finally had it ready to take to the publisher. On the way to the publisher, he stopped to buy something, leaving the manuscript in the car. When he came back, the manuscript was gone. It was his only copy. The event sent him into a downward spiral from which it took him years to recover. Perhaps the story is apocryphal and the professor was just a drunk. But it illustrates the point that Solomon is making here. A man who loses everything in a bit of bad business can be virtually destroyed by the event.

Thus ends Solomon's reflections on stuff. Stuff cannot be trusted. Stuff cannot be relied on. It is as apt to disappear as it is to appear. It is more apt to disappoint than to satisfy. In fact, it never really satisfies even if preserved, because the man who has stuff always wants more of it. Stuff is an evil master, and is really no profit at all, though it may seem to be so at the time.

12. Recommendation Redux

Ecclesiastes 5:18-19

[18] Also, every man to whom God gives riches and property, and gives power to eat from it and to receive his portion and to rejoice in his labour—this, it is the gift of God. [19] For he does not much remember the days of his life, for God occupies him with the joy of his heart.

In light of the preceding critique of stuff, Solomon again visits the question, What then is good in life? If the gathering of stuff does not satisfy; if stuff ultimately disappoints; if stuff ultimately leaves us naked in the face of death, then what is to be done? Solomon's recommendation is essentially a repeat of what he said at the end of chapter 2: eat, drink, and look for good in one's labour. This is the gift of God. All these things are in the hands of God and it is necessary for man to recognize and remember that. Stuff disappoints because it isn't God. Stuff disappoints because it cannot be relied on. It can disappear. It can be lost in a bad venture. It can leave one shamed before a watching world. God, on the other hand, does not disappoint. He can be relied on. One thing for which God can be relied on is the enjoyment of the small, ordinary things of life. These are the things we take for granted. But Solomon reminds us that we should not do so. These things are regular, small reminders of God at work in our lives. These things are allotted by God, and are to be received as gifts from his hand. Verse 18 (19) essentially repeats that idea, reminding the reader of the truth of the matter: 'Also, every man to whom God gives riches and property, and gives power to eat from it and to receive his portion and to rejoice in his labour.' Think about that. Some men have riches. Some men do not. Of those who have riches, some enjoy them and some do not. Of those without riches, some are content and some are not. Some men enjoy their labour. Others do not. But those who enjoy their labour are not just lucky. They haven't just picked the right occupation. They have received a gift from God. As for those who are rich, yes there has often been hard work involved, but ultimately it is a gift from God. Some men work hard and receive nothing, so those who have wealth need to remember that what they have is a gift of God.

Verse 19 (20): 'For he does not much remember the days of his life, for God occupies him with the joy of his heart.' The man described here is the man whom God has taught to number his days. He knows that his days are few. They come to an end. He will not live under the sun forever. So he enjoys the few days that he has. Such is the answer God gives to the cry of the man's heart. Men, because they are sinners, want more. They think they deserve more. The man who fears God realizes that he does not deserve more, he deserves less. So whatever he does have, he takes delight in it as a gift from God. May we all so respond to the simple gifts that God gives to us!

This verse can also be rendered, 'For he shall not much remember the days of his life, for God answers in the joy of his heart.' If taken in that sense, the fact that the days of a man's past fade away is a good thing. We often lament the vagaries of memory, but fail to recognize that God often delivers his people from memories of awful events and actions. On the other hand, some people are tortured by the inability to forget things that they would rather forget. There is another sense lurking here as well. That is, recognizing that God answers a man in the joy of his heart keeps a man looking forward. Rather than getting lost in the past, the gift of God can enable a man to keep looking to the future. This is the promise, for example, in 1 Thessalonians 4, where Paul encourages his readers to comfort one another with the reminder that the Lord is returning. In this sense, as bizarre as it may seem, Christians can encourage themselves and one another by remembering the future.

13. The Evil of Life

Ecclesiastes 6:1-9

¹ There is an evil I have seen under the sun, and it is heavy upon mankind. ² A man to whom God gives wealth and property and honour and there is no lack for his soul from anything which he desires, and God does not enable him to eat from it, for a foreign man eats it. This is vapour. It is an evil sickness. ³ If a man begets a hundred (children) and lives many years. And many were the days of his years, but his soul was not satisfied from the good, and also there was not burial for him, I said, better than him is the stillborn. ⁴ For in vapour it comes and in darkness it goes, and in darkness his name was covered. ⁵ Also, it did not see the sun and it did not know the quiet of either this or that. ⁶ Even if he lived a thousand years twice over, and he did not see good, do not all go to one place?

⁷ All the labour of a man is for his mouth, and also the soul is not filled. ⁸ For what advantage has the wise man over the fool? What is it to the poor knowing to walk before the living? ⁹ Better is the sight of the eyes than the walking of the soul. Also this is vapour and herding wind.

Solomon continues to press upon the reader the various injustices of life under the sun. He posits here again a man of wealth and substance who has all that he might desire, yet he does not enjoy it. Instead, another man (literally, a man, a stranger or foreigner) enjoys it. It is a little difficult to imagine the situation here. Two things strike me as possible. One is that the man acquires all that he desires, then dies before he has the opportunity to enjoy it. The other possibility is that perhaps he gains it all and then loses it to another man, such as through a bad business venture. Another possibility with this second option is that he gains all these things and then the land is overrun by a foreign power, and someone associated with that foreign power gets to enjoy all that this man had amassed. The possibility that the man dies before he can enjoy what he has acquired seems to fit better with the context, if he is being contrasted with the man in the following verses who lives an extraordinarily long life. In any case, this is vanity; that is, it is the result of living in a fallen world, where things do not always work out the way we wish them to. It is a sore evil. It vexes men.

Verse 3 seems to present a contrast. Here, the man has many children as well as amassing all the good things for which he longed (one assumes). He also lives an extraordinarily long life. Yet he is not satisfied. Here, the idea does not seem to be that he loses all that he has gained. Instead, it simply does not satisfy. He spends his long life yearning for more. Early death or long life: if a man is not satisfied with what he has, or cannot enjoy what he has, he is no better off than a miscarried child. In fact, in Solomon's view, the latter is better off. Why? Because he ends up in the same place as this man does but without all his trouble and heartache.

The mention of a thousand years twice over is probably a specific allusion to the lives of the antediluvian patriarchs. Since they only approached a thousand years, Solomon is proposing that someone who lives twice as long, even with the blessing of many children, still only experiences a miserable life if without satisfaction.

The reference in verse 3 to 'no burial' has raised some debate. Perhaps the more common view is that the man dies without being buried. In ancient Israelite culture (and in many other ancient cultures) a man who dies without being buried has received the ultimate insult. If this is how the verse is to be read, then the assertion is this: If a man has many children, and lives a long life, yet does not enjoy his things, and dies in humiliation, then a stillborn child is better off than he.

But there are two problems with this reading of the text. First, the focus seems to be on the degree of satisfaction experienced. If this is a reference to a humiliating death, that splits the focus. Second, there seems to be a deliberate contrast between this man and the man mentioned in verse 1. The man of verse 1 lacks the opportunity to enjoy his goods. In the case of the man in verse 3 he has the opportunity, but nonetheless does not enjoy his goods.

Perhaps the key to understanding what is being said here is the reference to 'no burial' as meaning that the man doesn't die. In other words, no matter how long a man lives (generally considered a good thing in itself), and no matter how many children he may have (also generally considered a good thing in itself), if such a man does not enjoy the good things he has, he would have been better off not to have been born at all.[1]

All men go to one place. That is, all die. It is better for a man to enjoy the good things he has while he has opportunity to do so. Ultimately, however, both the opportunity and the ability to enjoy good things are the gifts of God. That is the assertion of 5:17-19 (5:18-20), and that guides the understanding of these first several verses of chapter 6.

Solomon continues in the meditation on satisfaction in what follows. Verse 7 is probably a proverb: 'All the labour of the man is for his mouth, and yet the soul is not filled.' The contrast is between the satisfying of the physical appetite

---

[1] Reichert and Cohen, *The Five Megilloth*, p. 146.

and the satisfying of the spiritual appetite. The first can be accomplished, and must be accomplished if the man is to live. Yet the mere satisfying of the body will not satisfy the soul. Further, the soul is much harder to satisfy than the body. Solomon has much to say about satisfaction, most of it emphasizing the fact that man, living in a fallen world, is beset by dissatisfaction. It is one of the conundrums of life.

In this case, what advantage does the wise man have over the fool? The placing of the question here implies that it is related to the issue of satisfaction. Some take this to be a rhetorical question that implies that the wise man has no advantage over the fool. I take it otherwise. Solomon is rather implying the opposite. The wise man does have an advantage over the fool. The wise man will recognize that the opportunity and ability to enjoy the good are from the hand of God. Thus, the wise man will take advantage of those opportunities and abilities. The fool, on the other hand, does not understand that, and thus will miss the opportunity and will fritter away the ability to enjoy the good.

The second half of verse 8 is more difficult. Literally, it reads: 'What to the poor man who knows to walk before the living?' Given the context, presumably the word 'advantage' is implied in the sentence: 'For what advantage has the wise man over the fool? What is it to the poor knowing to walk before the living?' This also is usually taken as a rhetorical question expecting a negative answer: There is no advantage to the poor man who knows how to walk before the living.

However, it is possible that this line is to be understood in the fuller context, not only of the immediate verse, but of the preceding verses as well. In that case, it seems to me that the question, while being rhetorical, does not expect a negative answer. The implication in the context of the entire verse is this: as the wise man has the advantage over the fool, in that he understands he must not be controlled by his appetites, so the poor man who knows how to walk before the living (that is, he knows how to conduct himself in life) has the advantage over the fool. The fool does not know how to conduct himself, and is driven by his appetites, which are never satisfied. The poor man with understanding, however, has the advantage in that he sees things in their proper perspective. He knows how to conduct himself. He is not driven by his appetites. He 'has learnt to accommodate himself to his circumstances.'[2]

Verse 9 continues the thought of satisfaction and desire. The first half of the verse is the equivalent of 'A bird in the hand is worth two in the bush.' In other words, that which the eye beholds is contrasted with the (literally) walking about of the soul. The 'walking about' soul is the one that is not satisfied, it is the unsatisfied soul of verse 7.

This also is vanity and striving after wind, Solomon's repeated judgment on human behaviour. Many take this phrase as being the equivalent of 'This is pointless and futile.' The CEB, for example, translates it as, 'This too is pointless, just wind chasing.' But it is difficult to see how this understanding really fits the context. Instead, it appears to me to be Solomon's droll comment on human life in a fallen world. 'This is it. What more would you expect?' This may have the sound of cynicism, but in fact it is the clear-eyed realism that Solomon has been encouraging his readers to adopt. It is better to have than to want. Yet the desire of a man will always remain unsatisfied. Therefore, learning to be satisfied with what one has, learning how to behave oneself in the land of living under the sun is something to be desired. Learning to control one's appetite is the way of wisdom.

[2] Reichert and Cohen, *The Five Megilloth*, p. 147.

14. The Problem of Man

Ecclesiastes 6:10-12

¹⁰ What will be—its name has already been called. And it is known that he is man. And he is not able to contend with the one more powerful than he. ¹¹ When there are many words, vapour multiplies. What is the advantage to the man? ¹² For who knows what is good for the man in life the number of the days of his vaporous life? And he does them as a shadow. Whoever declares to the man what will be after him under the sun?

Verse 10. 'What will be—its name has already been called. And it is known that he is man. And he is not able to contend with the one more powerful than he.' Obviously, there is a change of subject here. It appears that now Solomon has moved again to a consideration of the control of God over all things. That which has come into being has already been named. Its character has been defined and determined. In particular, God is concerned with man. Man is a creature, with creaturely limitations. Some take 'who is mightier than he' as a reference to death. That seems unlikely from the context. Rather, God again is in view. He is mightier than man, and man might try, but is unable to contend successfully against God.

Verse 11. 'When there are many words, vapour multiplies. What is the advantage to the man?' Again, Solomon warns against the man of many words, since multiplying words only increases vanity. Another way of thinking about this verse is as follows: most of us know someone who talks too much. So what do we do when they begin talking? We simply tune them out. Their words go into the air and are lost. Nothing is gained by the multiplying of words. Solomon is implicitly recommending the benefit of few, well-chosen words over many words that simply dissipate in the air like one's breath on a cold morning. Men are not improved by the multiplication of words. 'Short and sweet' did not become a proverb without good reason!

Verse 12 is often taken as the complaint of the ignorant. Nobody knows what is good for man to do. There's no point to anything. No one knows what is coming. It is all useless. However, as we have already seen frequently in this book, that is not Solomon's view. These so-called negative statements, that allegedly depict the helplessness of man before an implacable universe, are usually to be understood positively. So here, in the context it has already been asserted that man cannot contend successfully with God. God has already determined what will be. He is the one calling all things into existence. Therefore, he is the one who knows what is good for man. He is the one who knows what comes next. So in the ephemerality that is man's life, man must look to God for direction as to how to spend his life and for future hope.

It is important, according to Solomon, for man to have a proper understanding of his place in the order of things. There is one who is more powerful than man, with whom man cannot contend. He is the one who calls all things into existence. Therefore, man is to look to him in order to know what it is that is good for man to do. The life of man is a brief shadow. We do not have much time here. Therefore it is especially urgent that we know what is the good for us to do.

That knowledge comes only from the one who called all things into existence, the only one who can declare what is to come.

At this point, the first half of the book comes to a conclusion. Solomon has set before us the world as he sees it in his divinely given wisdom. Human life in a fallen world is a passing shadow. As a result, it is filled with frustrations, injustices, inequities, and inexplicable difficulties. But in the midst of this, the wise man remembers that God is the Creator, that man is answerable to him, and that the wise man lives in the fear of God.

15. Proverbs Contrasting Wisdom and Folly

Ecclesiastes 7:1-12

¹ Better is a name than good oil and the day of death than the day of his birth.

² Better to go to the house of mourning than to go to the house of feasting, because it is the end of every man. And the living takes it to his heart.

³ Better is vexation than laughter, for in the evil of the face, the heart is good.

⁴ The heart of the wise is in the house of mourning and the heart of fools in the house of rejoicing.

⁵ Better to listen to the rebuke of the wise than for a man to listen to the song of fools. ⁶ For as the sound of thorns under the pot, thus is the laughter of fools. Even this is vapour.

⁷ For oppression makes mad the wise, and a bribe destroys the heart.

⁸ Better is the end of a matter than its beginning. Better is length of spirit [patience] than height of spirit [pride].

⁹ Do not rush in your spirit to be vexed, for vexation rests in the heart of fools.

¹⁰ Do not say, What has been in the former days was better than these. For it is not from wisdom that you ask this.

¹¹ Wisdom is good with an inheritance, and an advantage to those who see the sun.

¹² For in the shadow of wisdom, in the shadow of money. And the profit of knowledge is that wisdom gives life to its master.

At this point, the tone of the book changes. It begins to sound more like the book of Proverbs, though with a little mystery thrown in. Solomon has already established his foundation: live your brief life in the fear of God, enjoying the blessings of this life as God gives you the opportunity and the ability to do so. Now he begins to give practical advice, setting out what a life lived in the fear of God looks like. He does not begin where the reader of Proverbs might expect, but at a point that would not surprise the reader of Ecclesiastes: *the constant reminder of death*.

The parallel in the first verse might not seem obvious to the reader. The first line is almost a truism in Israelite wisdom literature. A good name, that is, a good character, is to be highly valued. The worth of a good name is greater than the worth of precious oil. But the second line is an unexpected parallel. It is likely that Solomon has in mind a connection between the two lines. A man's name, his character, can only be established at death. There are many saints in the Old Testament who began well, but ended poorly, so a final evaluation of a man's name must wait until his death. That is a stark reminder to Solomon's readers, once again reminding them of the inevitability of death.

The next few verses ring the changes on the theme of death as it relates to the wise man. The house of feasting and merry-making can mislead people, causing them to forget their mortality and the judgment that awaits them. But Solomon does not want his readers to be distracted. Go to the funeral, he says. That is your end as well. Do not forget it. Let it sit in your mind. As Jacob took to heart Joseph's dreams (Gen. 37) and as Mary treasured in her heart the things said about Jesus (Luke 2), so the wise man holds on to the ultimate truth of his own certain death. Though some translations render the beginning of verse 3 as 'frustration' (NIV) or 'aggravation' (CEB), the use of this word in Ecclesiastes is better represented by 'sorrow' (KJV, ESV, NLT) or 'grief' (CSB). This seems to be the meaning of the word throughout Ecclesiastes (see also 1:18; 2:23; 5:16; 11:10). This use of the word also fits better in the immediate context, where the reference has just been made to the house of mourning. Sorrow and grief remind us of the vanity of life, whereas joy distracts us from it.

The bluntness of the second line is typical of Proverbs: 'for in the evil of the face, the heart becomes good.' Some translations soften it (for example, NLT: 'for softness has a refining influence on us'). But part of the point of these statements is to make the reader stop and ask himself, 'Did I just read what I think I read?' Proverbs are meant to be mulled over. Softening translations enable us to read right past the hard sayings of the Bible.

The 'evil of the countenance' is a phrase that occurs also in Genesis 40:7.[1] Joseph comes upon the butler and the baker after their dreams and asks them why their countenance (face) is evil. They have both had dreams. They are troubled by the dreams, partly from the content of the dreams, and partly from the fact that they have a sense the dreams have meaning, but they don't know what that meaning is. Such events make us stop and take stock. Serious consideration produces fruit, and our hearts become better for it.

The reader needs to remember that 'heart' as referred to in the Old Testament is not the seat of emotion (though it has that sense occasionally); primarily it refers to the seat of the intellect. Thus, things and events that cause an evil countenance make us think. They improve our minds, our understanding.

[1] Reichert and Cohen, *The Five Megilloth*, p. 150.

That is the point of the house of mourning. It reminds us of our end, and the responsibility facing us.

The wise man thinks on the serious things of life, whereas the fool is always looking to be distracted. Just as an applicatory aside, I am not one in favour of a dour look and a lack of humour. But I do wonder what is going on in our thinking when 'but it was funny' becomes a justification for indulging all sorts of foul and wicked thoughts. I wonder when I hear a Christian justifying some vile (that is, bad morals, bad language, bad example) television show or movie by noting that *it was funny*. It makes me wonder about the sanctification of our minds.

Verse 5. Wise men want to be corrected. Fools want to be entertained. Verse 6 continues the thought with a different image. Imagine a person setting a pot on a fire. Under the pot he has gathered thorn bushes for fuel. The thorn bushes burn so quickly that the fire is unable to produce any real effect on the pot. That is the effect of the fool's laughter. It is here, then it is gone, and it has produced no real effect.

Verse 7. The word (*'osheq*) can mean oppression or extortion. Given the context here, the latter is probably preferable, because the parallel is clearly a bribe. Extortion turns a wise man into a fool, because he is forced into behaviour he would not otherwise countenance. In like fashion, a gift (bribe, also used in this sense in Prov. 15:27) destroys the mind. Such uses of power and money drive a wise man off course. Hence the wise man is advised to steer well clear of all such uses of power and money.

There are two aspects to be considered here. The first one is when the wise man is the weaker man in the interaction: that is, he is the one being extorted or bribed. In those cases, he is forced into actions that he knows are not wise, but has no choice. The other possibility is that the wise man is the extorter or briber. Such things can arise as temptations to him, because the wise man is often a successful man, and operates in positions of power. But Solomon warns against the temptation. The use of such things is corrupting. Not that he was a wise man, but the main character in the TV series *Breaking Bad* was a good example of someone corrupted by the temptation to use illicit means to gain his ends.

Verse 8. There is a common saying to the effect that it is not the end, but the journey that counts. There is some truth to the importance of the journey, but the end itself should not be discounted. That is Solomon's point here. The conclusion is important. It should also be noted that this line could be translated, 'Better is the end of a word than its beginning.'[2] If taken in that sense, the idea is that it is the result of a statement that matters. I am reminded here of something a friend told me: someone had spoken only a couple of sentences to her, but they meant a lot. They had really blessed her. The person who spoke those sentences was probably unaware of the effect that they had. That is often the case. We say something, not knowing its ultimate effect. All the more reason, then, that we should think carefully before we speak, so that the person to whom we speak might receive benefit.

In the second line of verse 8, there is a delightful image that simply doesn't make it into translations. It is usually translated along the lines of 'patience of spirit is better than haughtiness of spirit' (NASB). Or it is simplified further to 'Patience is better than arrogance' (CEB). The Hebrew reads, 'better is length of spirit than height of spirit.' The English versions have captured the meaning, but have lost the image in the process. The image itself is worth reflecting on. The word 'long' here is often used in the phrase 'long of anger' (for example, Prov. 14:29) where the idea is that of being slow to get angry. Thus a long spirit is a spirit with much patience. The word 'high' is often used in the sense of 'exalted' or 'haughty' (for example, Psa. 138:6, where it is contrasted with 'the lowly'). So

---

[2] Reichert and Cohen, *The Five Megilloth*, p. 151.

height of spirit is arrogance. But the concrete, spatial contrast increases the force of the proverb. The idea is further developed in verse 9, where the image shifts from height to speed. Do not hasten to be angry. Anger is a characteristic of fools (Prov. 12:16). The word can also mean 'vexation.' The fool is easily vexed. The wise man responds with greater equanimity. The wise man is self-controlled. The fool lacks that control, particularly of emotions. There is a sense in which anger and vexation are both characteristic of fallen man. The universe does not go along with our wishes, it vexes us. We respond with anger and frustration. That is the response of the fool, who is foolish in part because he does not understand the way things really are. The wise man, on the other hand, recognizes the true state of the world. Thus he is not much surprised by the inequities and injustices of the world. They are part of a fallen universe, and function, at least in part, to make us long for a perfected world.

We have set before us here two concerns, arrogance and anger. Both are shown to be characteristics of the fool. In our culture, we are often quick (pun intended) to criticize the adulterer, and rightly so. The adulterous or drunken minister is driven from office. But how many men are in that sense sober and faithful, yet quick to anger and arrogant as well. Yet they continue safely in their ministerial positions, doing untold damage along the way. Perhaps those who oversee ministerial training and the evaluation of prospective ministers should be as concerned about the sins of the spirit as they are about the sins of the flesh.

Dissatisfaction is the theme of verse 10. Here, it is dissatisfaction in the guise of nostalgia. It can be taken two ways. Either in the sense of a general nostalgia for better times (usually involving a false perception of the past). Or it can be taken in a personal sense, that is, 'Why am I having so much trouble now, when earlier life was much easier for me?'³ In either case, this relates to the vexation and anger of the preceding verses. It is the fool who is unhappy with his situation.

If we take the verse in the first, more general sense, the fool sees himself as the victim, with a right to feel vexed. He was born in the wrong time or in the wrong place. The universe is against him. 'God hates me,' is his thought, characterized not by a recognition of his true state before God, but by a sense that God has mistreated him. He deserves so much better from the Almighty. The wise man, on the other hand, recognizes that God has placed him in this precise time and place for his own sovereign purposes. The thing to do then is to seek how God would have us act in the here and now.

If we take the verse in the more specific sense of a man lamenting that things were previously better for him than they are now, vexation is again the response of the fool. He still sees himself as the victim. His only desire is to get out of the current situation. It is, in his mind, God's responsibility to do this. The response of the fool is well-illustrated in the stories of the people described in Philip Yancey's practical little book *Disappointment with God*. These are people who operated under the assumption that God owed them something. What that *something* was differed from person to person, but the sense of entitlement was the same. They were the victims. But really, they were the fools.

The wise man, on the other hand, knows that God has placed him in trying circumstances for his own good. He also recognizes that the previous days might not have been as pleasant as he remembers them. What Solomon is recommending here is a complacency, an equanimity in the face of the vicissitudes of life. The wise man recognizes that all things are in the hand of God. He fears God, trusting that the judge of all the earth will do right.

³ Reichert and Cohen, *The Five Megilloth*, p. 152.

Solomon sums up this line of thinking in verses 11-12, emphasizing the benefits of wisdom. Verse 11 says, 'Wisdom is good with an inheritance, and an advantage to those who see the sun.' Several translations have 'Wisdom is as good as an inheritance.' This is a tempting way to read the verse, but it is not clear that the preposition ever has the sense of 'as good as' instead of 'with.' Solomon's point here is not fiscal. He is not saying, 'Money (an inheritance) is good, but it is even better with wisdom.' Earlier in the book Solomon has on several occasions alluded to the problem of men who have raised a fortune but then must leave it to someone else, and they don't know what the inheritors will do with it. So Solomon's point here is that wisdom along with that inheritance prevents the inheritance from being wasted. That is why the second line says that it (wisdom) is a profit to those who see the sun. Wisdom is a help to navigating our way through life. It prevents foolish decisions. It preserves one's inheritance. This is not an idea to be scoffed at, but rather to be welcomed. Another way of making Solomon's point is that without wisdom, there is no advantage to the inheritance, because it will soon be gone.

Verse 12 is a somewhat cryptic restatement of the same idea. 'For in the shadow of wisdom, in the shadow of money. And the profit of knowledge is that wisdom gives life to its master.' The first line is generally translated as, 'For the protection of wisdom is like the protection of money' (ESV). It assumes that the juxtaposition of the two clauses implies a comparison. It also takes the concrete word 'shadow' as a metaphor for 'protection,' a sense that it sometimes has. However, the line can also, and I think preferably, be taken as related noun clauses making up one whole line, rather than two separate lines. Thus: 'For to be in the shadow of wisdom is to be in the shadow of money.' Solomon is not about to deny that money has advantages. It is the misuse or the foolish use of money that he fears. But here the fundamental idea is that money can provide protection (shade). There are many things that the man without money fears, because he does not have the protection that money would give him. Likewise, that man who has money does not worry about many things that concern the man who lacks the necessary financial resources. The poor man worries where his next meal will come from. The rich man does not. The man without money worries about the next rent payment. The man with money does not. In a similar fashion, the wise man is protected from many things that are a danger to the fool. In that sense, then, wisdom preserves the life of its owner. The wise man avoids the dangers of the fool, and by his wise preparation is protected from difficulties that overwhelm the fool in the end.

This section (7:1-12) focuses on the advantage of wisdom in this life. Earlier in the book, Solomon has made it clear that wisdom cannot answer all the questions of life under the sun. But that does not mean that wisdom does not have its uses. Wisdom gives perspective and order to the life of a man under the sun. It enables him to avoid the ditches into which the fool falls. But there are limits to wisdom. It is to those limits that Solomon next addresses himself.

16. The Limitations of Wisdom

Ecclesiastes 7:13-29

¹³ Consider the work of God. For who is able to straighten that which he has made crooked?

¹⁴ In the day of good, be good. And in the day of evil, consider: even the one as the other God has made, so that the man will not find out anything after him.

¹⁵ I have seen everything in my vaporous days. There is a righteous man who perishes in his righteousness, and there is a wicked man prolonged in his wickedness. ¹⁶ Do not be too much righteous and do not make yourself excessively wise. Why should you ruin yourself? ¹⁷ Do not be too much wicked and do not be ignorant. Why should you die before your time? ¹⁸ It is good that you should seize on this and on that. Do not let your hand rest. For the one who fears God goes out with all of them.

¹⁹ Wisdom gives strength to the wise more than ten rulers who were in the city.

²⁰ For there is no man righteous on the earth who does good and does not sin.

²¹ Also, to all the words that they speak, do not set your heart, so that you do not hear your servant cursing you. ²² For even many things your heart knows, that also you have cursed others.

²³ All this I tested with wisdom. I said, I will be wise.

And it was far from me. ²⁴ What has been is distant and exceedingly deep. Who can find it out?

²⁵ And once again I turned my heart, to know and to search out and to seek wisdom and thought, and to know the wickedness of stupidity and the nonsense of madness. ²⁶ And I was finding more bitter than death the woman whose heart is snares and traps. Her hands are fetters. The one who is good before God escapes from her and the sinner is captured by her. ²⁷ Consider this that I have found, Qohelet said. I have added one thing to another to find out the conclusion. ²⁸ What my soul seeks I did not find. One man among a thousand I found and a woman among all these I did not find. ²⁹ Only consider this that I found: God made man upright, but they have sought out many devices.

Verse 13 takes us immediately back to 1:15, where Solomon first began his investigation of wisdom. His conclusion then was that wisdom was incapable of bringing full understanding to the ultimate questions. So the reader needs to take that hint at this point in the book as well. Solomon is shifting from considering the usefulness of wisdom to considering its uselessness, or perhaps better, its limitations.

To begin with, Solomon wants the reader to see (the literal meaning of the word translated 'consider') the work of God. As a side note, the imperative here is translated as 'consider' in most English versions. In one sense, there is nothing wrong with that. That is the sense of the word in this place, and it occurs in this sense in many places in the Old Testament. But there is a concreteness to 'see' that is lost by the more abstract 'consider.' Look around. See the work of God. There's no fixing it. There's no changing it. If he has made it crooked, it cannot be straightened.

Now Solomon begins to show how, even with its limitations, even recognizing that the work of God cannot be undone, nor 'fixed,' wisdom can be helpful in navigating life under the sun. 'In the day of good, be good.' This is really what Solomon has been recommending in his summary conclusions. Enjoy what you can when you can. This is not Epicurean indulgence. It is wisely taking advantage of those gifts that God gives when he gives them. 'And in the day of evil, consider.' There's that word again. Don't be afraid to look at life. Recognize that God has made the good day alongside the bad day. But Solomon wants the reader to consider more than this. God has not acted randomly in this. Instead he has done it with purpose. His purpose is, as it were, to keep man in the dark. So that man cannot find anything after him. By looking at the past and the present, men attempt to predict the future. And in some general sense they may be able to have an inkling of what is coming. But only in the most general sense. For example, apparently no one really saw World War I coming. No one really saw the Great Depression coming. No one really saw the recent Great Recession coming. Man simply does not have adequate resources of wisdom to produce the necessary insight. But Solomon's consideration here is not just with man generically. Rather, it is with man specifically: a man. A man cannot find out what comes after him. God has made it this way on purpose. The reader might resent that truth. But he has to conclude that Solomon is right. We do not know in the morning what the evening will bring. We do not know at the beginning of the year how the year will end. All these things come upon us unknown and unexpected, and they do so by the design of God.

Solomon then moves to consider other conundrums unsolvable by human wisdom. These things are in the hand of God, but we cannot figure them out. These are things that Solomon has seen under the sun—in the days of his brief, passing life.

Verse 15. Solomon has 'seen it all' during his brief life. That serves as the title to this section. He then begins to list and comment on some of the things he has seen (and considered). The first of these is the inequity that he has witnessed.

A righteous man dies young and a wicked man dies old. Obviously, this does not always happen. But it happens often enough that it deserves comment.

Verses 16-17 are a commentator's nightmare. This appears to be what Solomon is recommending: on the one hand be neither too righteous, nor too wise; on the other hand, be not too wicked, nor be foolish. As I have said, this causes a great deal of consternation among commentators. But is there a way of understanding this recommendation that does not undercut the pursuit of righteousness?

First, we have to consider the context. Solomon has moved from some practical uses of wisdom in verses 1-12 to some difficulties that wisdom cannot solve in verses 13-29. So the underlying emphasis of this section is that wisdom cannot solve all the problems that man faces. Some things are simply inexplicable.

Second, he has started this little section with the comment that some righteous men die young, and some wicked men die old. This is an anomaly, especially in the Old Testament covenantal context, where righteousness, defined as a general faithfulness to the law, results in long life, while wickedness brings on the judgment of God. In light of that, Solomon's recommendation is a *via media*. Remember that wisdom cannot solve all problems, so don't devote yourself to wisdom overmuch. Also remember that all die, so a striving for perfect righteousness in this life will not produce everlasting existence in this life. Accept that perfection cannot be achieved in this life. However, do not let that understanding lead you into wickedness and folly, for those are surely deadly. Another way of putting it might be: 'Don't be too hard on yourself.' There does not seem to me to be in this anything contrary to New Testament teaching on practical righteousness. Verse 18 then instructs us to hold on to both of these things at the same time.

It is the same conundrum that Paul deals with in Romans 6. If God is glorified in saving sinners, let us sin all the more.

No! The New Testament letters make it clear that righteousness must be considered under two heads. First, there is the absolute righteousness that the sinner has in Christ in justification. This cannot be added to, nor subtracted from. But then there is the practical righteousness. We are told to pursue holiness, without which no man shall see God. But perfection in this righteousness (holiness) will not be achieved in this life. It is a necessary recognition if a Christian is to live with himself and with others.

The other side of the matter is that we should not become complacent and indulgent with our sin (wickedness). That is the path of folly, and it is deadly. This is indeed a fine line. It is difficult to keep both these ideas together at the same time, and live in the light of them. That is why, in verse 19, Solomon says that wisdom gives strength to the wise. It requires a really wise man to recognize this twofold truth—we must pursue righteousness, while recognizing that it is an unattainable goal in this life. It is only the truly wise man who can apprehend, and adapt himself to, the limits of wisdom. Such wisdom is better than a city with ten (presumably wise) rulers. Solomon concludes this paragraph by reminding the reader that there is not a man who does good and never sins. This reasserts the context for the *via media* statement in verses 16-17.

Verses 21-22. Don't pay attention to everything you hear. And don't be disturbed when you hear disagreeable things about you come out of your servant's mouth. You know that you yourself have done the same thing many times. Here, Solomon reminds his readers that we are all in the same boat. We are guilty of sins of the tongue. As a result, we should not be too hard on others when we hear them commit those same sins. Solomon's advice here is sound. For our tendency is to hold others to a much stricter account that we hold ourselves. One can easily imagine the overheard slave getting sacked for his remarks, while the owner who sacks him blithely forgets or ignores his own like transgressions.

Verses 23-29 are something of a wrap-up for the whole section. Solomon starts off by saying that he has tested all these things by wisdom. That is, he has subjected them to thorough investigation. He has turned them over completely in his mind. He has looked at them from all sides. His conclusion is that true and full wisdom was beyond his grasp. It was far from him. There were things that his wisdom, great as it was, simply could not grasp. There were things too deep and too far off to take hold of. Solomon here is reminding the reader that human wisdom is not capable of solving all the problems and difficulties that lie before it. Many commentators take the view that Solomon is rejecting traditional Israelite wisdom. He is not. Rather, he is pointing out that it has its limits. Human beings are limited, and so is their wisdom.

Echoing 1:13 again, Solomon points out that he had set himself to examine all these things. As before, he concludes that wickedness is foolish and that folly is madness. Wisdom might not be able to solve all questions, but these things wisdom is clear about.

Verses 26-28 constitute a notoriously difficult passage. Most interpreters find here more than a little sexism or misogyny on the part of Solomon. Then they either condemn it, or they excuse it on the basis of Solomon's times, or on his personal experience, or both. Either approach strikes me as unhelpful. This is, after all, inspired literature. As such, it does not misrepresent the truth. Let us see if a re-examination of the passage in the larger context can help.

The context of this part of chapter 7 is set out to show those areas in which the wisdom of man is inadequate to understand, or to figure out the issues of life. In verse 23, for example, Solomon has said that he sought wisdom, but it was unattainable. There are many things that even the wisest of men cannot understand or explain. The section ends by reiterating the fallenness of man. God created him upright, but he has sought out many devices. Verse 25 reminds us that

Solomon understands the difference between wisdom and folly. Further, folly is madness, though it might be common. In that context, then, he is faced with a conundrum. As bitter as death is (and for Solomon it is certainly bitter, because it is the end of life under the sun), there is something he has found that is more bitter yet. That is the woman whose heart is snares and nets, and whose hands are bonds. The details of the language differ, but the image projected is that of the evil or adulterous woman that we find in the Book of Proverbs.[1] See, for example, the extended account in chapter 7. In the first nine chapters of Proverbs, there are repeated warnings against the adulteress. While it is true that Solomon is certainly warning young men to stay away from women who are adulteresses or prostitutes, there is a second, greater significance to these warnings. In the context of Proverbs 1-9, such women stand as figures of Folly (something made specific in 9:13). Thus, the young men are warned not only to stay away from marital infidelity, they are warned to stay away from folly. Folly is, in a certain sense, the opposite of faith or the fear of the Lord. Thus, the adulterous woman becomes a figure for foolishness. Falling for the adulteress, as did the young man in Proverbs 7, is the height of folly. Solomon, in Ecclesiastes 7:25, points out that folly is madness. So here, the image of the grasping, binding woman is an image of Folly. The second half of the verse is especially important here. The one who is good before the Lord escapes her, whereas the sinner is ensnared by her. As we have previously noted, 'good before the Lord' and 'sinner' are not so much moral categories in Ecclesiastes as they are indicators of those who, on the one hand, have received God's favour, and on the other hand, those who have not. So it is the fool who falls into the trap of the adulteress, whether that is taken in the literal or figurative sense that is probably being emphasized here. As the psalm says, the fool says in his heart

---

[1] This approach to the passage was brought to my attention from Tremper Longman in his Cornerstone commentary on Ecclesiastes.

that there is no God. He rejects wisdom and ends up in the bonds of folly.

Verses 27-29 are closely interconnected. The key word in these verses is 'find,' which occurs six times in the three verses. Three times, it has to do with finding and three times it has to do with not finding. The section begins with his announcement of finding: he has added one thing to another in order to find the account. Some translations (ESV, NIV) take it as 'scheme' (no doubt relating it to the word at the end of verse 29) but I think the idea here is mathematical, though it is connected with wisdom. He has searched, adding one thing to another, to find out the sum of wisdom. But there is something that he is yet seeking, that he has not yet found out. One man among a thousand he has found, but a woman among all of these he has not found. I don't think Solomon here is indulging in what our generation calls 'sexism.' I think his statement is more simple than that. What he has found is that one man among a thousand he has been able to understand, but he does not understand women at all. For those words to come from the pen of a man who had so much experience with so many women ought to give the rest of us pause for thought. Verse 29 gives the reason for this inability to understand people: God made man upright, but man has sought out many devices or schemes.

In the end, Solomon gives his ultimate conclusion, the best explanation he has for the behaviour of the human race. That is, though God made man upright, they went after their own devices. This statement clearly reflects Solomon's dependence on Genesis 1-3. God did make man upright, but the race has sought out its own understandings. This word *chishabon*, usually translated 'devices,' 'schemes,' or 'inventions,' is related to the word at the end of verse 27. Thus, I take it to be something like 'understanding.' That is, as the tree was able to make one wise (Gen. 3:6), men have sought out their own wisdom.

In chapter 7, Solomon has presented us with two images, both dependent on the proverb. The first image is a set of illustrations of what human wisdom is capable of. The second image sets forth those things that human wisdom simply cannot grasp. With these two images, he sets the stage for his discussion of those things that human wisdom can be used for. Chapter 7: understanding and lack of understanding. Chapter 8: the usefulness of what man can understand.

17. The Practical Use of Wisdom

Ecclesiastes 8:1-17

[1] Who is as the wise, and who knows the interpretation of a thing? The wisdom of a man gives light to his face and the strength of his face is changed. [2] As for me, watch the mouth of the king [keep the command of the king] on account of the oath of God. [3] Do not rush out from his presence. Do not stand in an evil matter. Whatever he delights in, he does. [4] Because the word of the king is authority and who will say to him, What are you doing? [5] Keep the commandment. Do not acknowledge an evil thing. The heart of the wise knows time and judgment. [6] For to every purpose there is a time and a judgment. For the evil of the man is much upon him. [7] For he does not know what will be. For just as it will be, who can declare to him? [8] There is no man ruling over the wind to restrain the wind. And there is no authority over the day of death. And there is no sending away in the battle. And the wicked will not rescue his master. [9] All this I have seen and given my heart to all work that is done under the sun: that the man has power over the man to his evil.

[10] And thus I have seen the wicked buried. And they came from the holy place. And they walked about and they were forgotten in the city where thus they had acted. Even this is vapour. [11] Because the sentence of the deed

of the wicked is not done quickly, therefore the heart of the sons of man is full in them to do evil. [12] Because the sinner does evil a hundred [times] and prolongs [his life], even this I know: that it will be good for those who fear God, who fear his presence. [13] And good shall not be to the wicked. And he shall not prolong days as a shadow who does not fear the presence of God.

[14] There is a vapour that is done upon the earth: that there are righteous treated according to the deed of the wicked, and there are wicked treated as the deed of the righteous. I said that this is vapour. [15] And I myself commended the joy that there is nothing better for the man under the sun but to eat and to drink and to rejoice, and it will accompany him in his labour the days of his life which God gives to him under the sun.

[16] Just as I gave my heart to know wisdom and to see the business that is done upon the earth that both by day and by night sleep with his eyes he does not see. [17] And I have seen all the work of God: that the man is not able to find out the deed that is done under the sun on account of which the man labours to seek, and he does not find out. And even if the wise man says he knows, he is not able to find out.

Chapter 7 covers both what human wisdom can and cannot accomplish. In chapter 8, Solomon begins to present some of the practical uses of wisdom, applying wisdom to a number of different situations. He begins by making the point that wisdom is a good thing. It is good to be wise. The first line of verse 1 is 'Who is like the wise man?' Some translations omit the implied comparison. So, for example, the NLT has, 'How wonderful to be wise.' But there is, as I said, an implied comparison here that is lost in the NLT. Much better, though still something of a paraphrase, is the NJB, 'Who compares with the sage?' With this implied comparison, Solomon elevates the wise man. Those interpretations of the book that hold Solomon denigrates wisdom are simply wrong on this point. Wisdom is good. Solomon's concern, though, is that wisdom is not, as it were, omnipotent. He follows this question with another rhetorical question, 'Who knows the interpretation of a thing?' The implied answer is that the wise man does. That is one of the benefits of wisdom. It allows one to understand and interpret matters that come to one's attention. While wisdom will not solve all riddles, it will solve many, and it is to be valued for that.

The next line might well be a proverb. 'The wisdom of a man gives light to his face and the strength of his face is changed.' This is the only place that the phrase, 'the strength of his face' occurs. So a little contemplation is necessary to decide what precise idea the image is intended to convey. BDB suggests 'boldness' or 'impudence.' The most common sense of the first word is 'strength' or 'might.' Thus, on reflection, the idea is probably more that of confidence, or certainty, rather than boldness. That is, the benefits of wisdom are comprehension (light) and confidence (strength). The man without wisdom also lacks understanding. Thus, when faced with a problem, he is at his wits' end, not knowing what to do, whereas the wise man has understanding, and can puzzle out the problem. Likewise, a man without wisdom, when faced with a difficult choice, may simply feel his way along, without any confidence that he has made the right choice. As a result, his progress is slow and uncertain. The wise man, however, can see through to the essence of the problem or the choice and thus move forward with confidence.

Verse 2 is a bit of a problem. Literally, it says, 'I the mouth of the king keep, and upon the matter of the oath of God.' Hence, the KJV adds 'counsel thee' after 'I.' The NASB adds 'say' after 'I.' Other translations drop the 'I' altogether. Another way of approaching the verse is to take the 'I' in the sense of 'as for me.' The personal pronouns are often used in this sense when beginning a clause. As for 'the mouth of the king,' mouth is often used in the sense of 'statement' or 'command.' For example, in Numbers 35:30 the phrase 'evidence of witnesses' (NASB) is literally 'mouth of witnesses.' More immediately pertinent is 1 Samuel 15:24, where 'command of the Lord' (NASB) is literally 'the mouth of the Lord.' So the first half of the verse says, 'As for me, watch the mouth of the king.' The second half of verse 2, while cryptic, is also not that difficult. It gives the reason for keeping the king's command. The preposition 'al often has the sense 'because of.' So read the second half of the verse, 'and because of the matter of the oath of God' (or 'on account of the oath of God.') It isn't good English, but it makes good sense. The man serving the king has taken an oath before God to do so. Therefore, it is incumbent upon him to obey the king, to follow his commands.

Solomon is lining out a particular area in which wisdom comes in handy, that is, when dealing with kings. The sense of verses 2-4 is that wisdom tells you to deal carefully and respectfully with kings. Verse 3 again has the terse, cryptic style of the proverb. Literally, 'Do not be hasty from his presence you go. Do not stand in an evil matter, for all that he desires he does.' There are a couple of different possibilities for the first line. It could mean that you are not to act impulsively by disassociating yourself from the king. That is, if you think the king has made a bad decision, do not resign your position in a huff. Be patient. Stick around. Perhaps you can be of help in correcting the course that the king has taken. Another possibility is that, when the king sends you on an errand, do not hasten out of his presence before you have heard the full order. Many times underlings have done something they thought the king desired because they hastened out of his presence, either literally or figuratively. That is, they may have stopped listening before the king stopped talking. As for 'Do not stand in an evil thing,' more than one possible understanding presents itself. One possibility is that it means 'Don't take part in something evil' (GWN). Another possibility is, 'Don't take a stand contrary to the king's wishes.' Another is, 'Don't persist in pursuing a bad course.' This clause is probably to be taken with the following clause. In that case it, the recommendation of the second clause may be as simple as 'don't get in the king's way, since he will get his way anyway.' Remember that this is instruction given to the wise. The wise man must understand that one handles the king with kid gloves. This, I think, is confirmed by verse 4. This verse confirms the end of verse 3. The king's word has power, and no one may question his decisions. One must remember that in most of the ancient world, the king's word was law. The king himself was not subject to law. Therefore, whatever the king commanded was to be obeyed.

Verse 5 directs the wise man to two things. First, he must reflect simple obedience to the law. Here *mitzvah* (law) is probably an allusion to the Law of Moses. Though the word *torah* is commonly connected with the Law of Moses, *mitzvah* occurs frequently throughout the Pentateuch as a synecdoche for the whole law. Some commentators think that there are no allusions to the Law of Moses in the book. I think this is clear evidence otherwise.

Other commentators, and some translations, take this as an expansion of the preceding verses and that it thus refers to the commandment of the king. The NASB, for example, reads, 'He who keeps a royal command.' However, when *mitzvah* is used in reference to a human command, that is usually made clear in the context. While it is true that this verse continues in the train of thought set by the preceding verses, it appears to me that Solomon's point is that a wise man keeps the command of God. In doing so, he will avoid evil. To follow the command of God is always a wise path. As Paul observes, against such there is no law.

The second line of the verse seems to me to follow the same idea. The heart of a wise man knows time and judgment. The word 'judgment' is a word that occurs frequently in the law of Moses. It frequently, though not always, refers to what we would call 'case law': if such and such happens, then thus and such should be done. Another way of putting it is to say that the wise man understands the appropriate time as well as the appropriate law for a particular consideration. An example might help here. 'God works all things together for good' is certainly a true statement. But it is probably not wise to quote it to someone who has just lost a family member in a tragic accident. The wise man knows the right law as well as the right time. Another way of thinking about it is to consider the wise man as a counsellor to the king. In providing counsel, he will seek to guide the king according to the law of God. He will select the right time and the right law when giving his advice to the king.

Verse 6 goes on to emphasize the point, by alluding to chapter 3:1. For every matter there is a time and a judgment. As that passage spoke about times, so this passage speaks about being able to recognize the times and to exercise judgment that is appropriate to it. The reason such wisdom is needed is because the evil of man is great upon him. In other words, there is great evil in the world. Men are capable of exercising great evil. The wise man will counter that evil by judicious use of the law. Another way of taking this second line is in the sense that there are many possible evil outcomes to a particular situation. The wise man seeks to avoid those outcomes by a careful and timely application of the law.

Verse 7 continues the thought by making the point that even the wise man does not know the outcome of events. He may plan and act toward a certain end, but he does not know if the end at which he aims is the end that will occur. Furthermore, there is no one who can tell him what will happen, or when it will happen. In short, the man who depends on only his own wisdom and insight is a fool, because he cannot know what he needs to know in order to achieve good ends. The wise man follows the commands of God, because God knows the end of a thing from its beginning. Things still may not work out the way the wise man hopes they will, but he is assured that he, by following the law, has acted in a judicious manner.

Verse 8 continues to deal with man's inability. Oddly enough, one does not usually think of a recognition of inability as a practical use of wisdom. But indeed it is. The man who recognizes his inabilities has a firm grasp on reality, something that Solomon is trying to inculcate to his readers. 'A man's got to know his limitations.'[1] Man can't control the wind. He can't control the day of his death. (Solomon is not including suicide in his consideration here.) These are truisms that people nonetheless tend to forget when they lose sight of their limitations.

The next line of the verse is a notoriously difficult one. It says, 'there is no sending away in war.' The word 'sending away' occurs only here and in Psalm 78:49, where it refers to God sending messengers of evil (evil angels) in judgment against his people. This does not really help in understanding this line in its context. One common interpretation is that the verse refers to the practice of sending someone in one's place to serve in the military. However, such a practice was common in the past. The wealthy could hire poor men to serve in their place when called upon to engage in warfare. The verse explicitly denies that, saying, there is no sending away. Another common view is that it means that no leave is granted in the midst of the battle. While true, this does not seem to fit the context. If we consider the context, that might give us some help. The first two lines express man's inability. He cannot control the wind. He cannot control the day of his death. The last clause says that wickedness cannot deliver its master. That is, there is really no benefit to being wicked. Implicitly, acting wickedly is an ordinary reaction on the part of fallen man. Men often take some evil action because they are under the impression that it will benefit them. Solomon denies that

[1] Dirty Harry in the movie *Magnum Force*.

benefit, again underscoring his larger point that the wise man not only knows his limitations, he knows that the law of God guides us profitably. So we have a context in which Solomon calls the reader to consider his inabilities, and to remind him that wickedness will not benefit him. One thing else of note. It says, 'there is no sending away in the battle.' That is, a specific battle is in view. Perhaps it means that there is no escape from the difficulties engendered by our inability. The last clause then is a reminder to the reader that acting wickedly will not deliver one from his inability and its results.

Verse 9 appears to introduce a new section. The 'all this' refers to what follows, not what precedes. That is, Solomon is saying, I have studied the following things, and these are my conclusions. He has studied all things done under the sun. One particular thing that he has studied, that is, he has observed it and meditated on it, namely the fact that there are times when one man has power over another to the 'evil' of the one under power. This could apply to any sort of oppression. Oppression is a natural part of a fallen world. Solomon has already commented extensively on the issue of oppression. While there might be times and places where oppression of various kinds is ameliorated, it cannot be removed from a fallen world. Solomon says no more about the issue here. He simply remarks on it as a part of his outline of ways in which wisdom has practical uses. In this particular case, the use of wisdom is to recognize the constancy of oppression. It does not occur in the same way or in the same area at all times, but it does occur as a regular element of life under the sun.

A second thing that he has observed and meditated on is the anomaly of the forgetting of the wicked dead. This verse has received some debate in the commentaries, so a little more discussion is in order. A painfully literal translation is: 'and in thus I saw wicked men buried. And they had entered, and from the holy place they had gone, and they were forgotten in the city in which thus they acted. Also this is vanity.' The key element here is the word 'forgotten.' The LXX translated this word as 'praised.' The difference between 'forgotten' and 'praised' is the shape of one letter. The two words could easily be confused. So what did Solomon write? Did he write that they were forgotten, or that they were praised? Either one would make sense in the context. The ESV has 'praised.' The NASB has 'forgotten.' If the NASB is right, the sense of the verse is probably accurately reflected by the NJB, 'forgetting how the wicked used to behave.' If the ESV is correct, the sense is that after wicked men die, they are praised. Either one is a frustration. The praising of wicked men after their death is the result of forgetting the fact of their wicked behaviour. Solomon is reminding the reader that the wickedness of the wicked (and the righteousness of the righteous) needs to be remembered, not forgotten. It is the forgetting of their wickedness that leads men to praise them after their death. But this is vanity. This is the experience of life under the sun. The verse looks back to 1:11. Solomon recognizes that there is no fixing this fact. But it is the role of wisdom to help one remember that this is reality.

Verses 11-15 constitute something of a summary section. Verse 11 deals with a legal problem that has been common in all ages. A decree (the word is a Persian loanword which probably came into Hebrew vocabulary as a result of Solomon's extensive trading throughout the Near East), meaning some legal statement, is not done quickly. As a result of delayed justice, men are encouraged in their wickedness. Judgment is not carried out against the law-breaker in a timely fashion, so the wicked presume that it will not be carried out at all. Again, it is a fact of life under the sun. It does not mean that justice should not be pursued. It does not mean that legal decrees should not be carried out in a timely manner. It does not mean that those in power should lack diligence in carrying out their work. It does mean, however, that these things happen, and that not infrequently. The wise man will recognize that fact, and know that sometimes one has to live with these things.

However, Solomon does not want to encourage any wicked man in adopting the thinking that justice will not be carried out. His assertion in verse 12 is the assertion of faith. The God-fearer, those people of faith, ought not to be discouraged by this apparent injustice. Even if a wicked man lives a long time, it is better to be one of those who fear God. The reader needs to remember that especially in the Old Testament, under the law of Moses, long life was a sign of blessing, built into the promises of the law. Thus, seeing someone live a long life tended to be taken as a statement of divine approval of their lives. Solomon is directing his reader here not to think in that way. It is the kind of thinking that argues from the results to the cause. I call it 'karma theology.' It was the theology of Job's friends. It was the theology of the Pharisees. It was the theology of the disciples in John 9: 'Who sinned? This man or his parents that he was born blind?' Such theology is profoundly mistaken, because it fails to recognize that there might be any number of causes leading to a particular result. Solomon here is saying that the wise man will not be misled by such thinking, but will remember that the fear of God is the beginning of wisdom, that is, the fear of God is the foundation of true wisdom. The God-fearer, or to use New Testament language, the person of faith, will truly benefit from his fear of God, even though that benefit might not be obvious at the time. Furthermore, even though the wicked man lives a long time, ultimately it will not go well with him. The wicked will not lengthen his days like the shadow. Solomon is playing here on the idea of lengthening one's days. In verse 12, he says that even if a wicked man lengthens his days, it is better to be a God-fearer. In verse 13, he says that the wicked will not lengthen his days. So which is it? Will the wicked man lengthen his days or not? The key is in the phrase 'like the shadow.' Again, Solomon is playing on words. Shadow can mean a place of safety, as in the shadow of God's wings. Or it can be an image of transitoriness. Or it can be an image of what is only a seeming reality. All three of these ideas come together in these two verses. The days of the wicked man who lives long are only shadow days. They are shadow, not substance. They are fleeting. Even if those days grow long as the shadow grows long, they are still brief. And the fundamental reason is that he does not fear God. There is no implicit promise here to the man of faith about a long life, but there is an implicit promise of a life that is more than a shadow.

In verse 14, Solomon moves on to another point: sometimes, righteous men get what it seems the wicked deserve, and sometimes the wicked seem to get what the righteous deserve. In other words, there is a lack of discernible justice in the way things work out in a fallen world. Thus the conclusion that this is vanity, this is how life is in a fallen world. The wise man recognizes this fact, and accepts it as a fact of life. Again, Solomon is not counselling complacency in the face of injustice. He is, however, calling on people to recognize and understand the fundamentally disordered state of the reality we inhabit. While injustices may be mitigated, and in some cases removed, it is not possible to remove, or even mitigate, all injustices.

In verse 15, Solomon reaches another of his fundamental recommendations. Most translations begin this verse with 'So I commend,' or 'So I recommend.' There is a problem with this rendering. First, a little background. There is a common conjunction in Hebrew that is generally translated 'and.' (If you read the KJV Old Testament, every time there is an 'and,' it probably reflects this conjunction.) It has a wide variety of uses, and is not always best translated by 'and.' The 'so' here is right. It indicates the consequence of the preceding observations. Another way of putting it is, 'as a result,' or 'in consideration of the preceding.' But the 'commend' or 'recommend' is weak. The verb is not a common word, but it is used a number of times in the Psalms, usually translated 'praise.' It is also used in Ecclesiastes 4:2, where the KJV translates it 'praised.' In that verse, the word has a certain shock value, because Solomon says he praised the dead. Here, Solomon is certainly making a recommendation. But it is stronger than that. He is encouraging, he is urging his readers to joy. In light of all the preceding frustrations and difficult truths of life in a fallen world, Solomon is saying, 'Go out and be joyful!' The reader is to enjoy his food and his drink and his happy times. There is nothing better for him under the sun than to do this. Rather than be grim and frustrated and sour, enjoy yourself! Remember that it is the gift of God, but enjoy yourself. Furthermore, don't just be joyful on rare occasions. Let joy accompany you throughout your life. Let it be your companion in your labour. Because this is the life God has given you. This statement is very close to that of Psalm 118:24. No one said being joyful would be easy, but all of this life is the gift of God. It is the wise man, it is the God-fearer who recognizes that fact and can thus properly rejoice in the life God has given him, however difficult it might be.

Verse 16. 'Just as I gave my heart to know wisdom and to see the business that is done upon the earth that both by day and by night sleep with his eyes he does not see.' The first line is clear, and is a repetition of things Solomon has said earlier. He has set himself to examine these things and to come to conclusions about them, that he might then recommend to others. The second line, however, is more difficult. It has been variously translated. Some translations, such as the KJV and the NASB, take it as a parenthetical remark about the ceaseless-ness of the investigation. Other translations (ESV and NLT) do not put it in parentheses, and consider it part of what Solomon is investigating. But let us look at it in the context of the following verse as well. Here Solomon is stating his conclu-sion. He saw all the work of God. And he saw that man is not able to figure out the work of God. So how does sleeplessness relate to both the seeking and the finding out? It might be that the KJV is right here. That Solomon is carrying out, or at least bringing into consideration, a ceaseless investigation. But that would seem to imply that the possessive pronoun on 'eyes' should be 'mine' not 'his.' The result of this view could be paraphrased as, 'I set my heart to know wisdom, without allowing my eyes to see sleep.'

A third option is that reflected in the NIV, that the sleeplessness is the very work that Solomon is investigating. In other words, this clause is expanding on the business that is done on the earth. And Solomon observes that it is true busyness. Man is busy day and night. If Solomon made that observation in his day, how much more today with our 24/7 news cycle, and business and life cycle. Fast food restaurants are often open 24 hours a day. You can place orders online 24/7.

Another possibility is that the business Solomon is referring to is that of God, and he observes that the work of God is not hindered by his requiring sleep.

In verse 17, Solomon turns to consider the work of God. He concludes that it is beyond man's comprehension. Even if a man labours at it, or is wise, it is still beyond his knowing.

So, the wisest man who ever lived has surveyed the work of God and has concluded that the totality of it is incomprehensible to man. The final practical use of wisdom that Solomon sets out here is the reminder that wisdom makes a man aware of his limitations.

18. In Light of the Limits of Wisdom

Ecclesiastes 9:1-17

¹ But all this I have given to my heart to find out all this: that the righteous and the wise and their servants are in the hand of God. Whether love or hate the man does not know everything before him. ² To all as to all, one fate. To the righteous, to the wicked, to the good and to the clean and to the unclean, and to the one who sacrifices and to the one who does not sacrifice, as the good as the sinner, the one who swears just as the one who fears to swear. ³ This is an evil in all that is done under the sun: that one fate happens to all. And also the heart of the sons of man is full of evil and madness in the heart while they live, and after him, to the dead. ⁴ For whoever is joined to all the living there is hope. For to be a living dog it is better than to be a dead lion. ⁵ For the living know that they will die, and the dead know not anything. And there is no more reward for them, for their memory is forgotten. ⁶ Also their love, their hate, their jealousy already has perished and there is no portion to them any more forever in all which is done under the sun.

⁷ Go, eat with joy your bread, and drink with a good heart your wine. For already God is pleased with your deeds.

⁸ At all times let your garments be white, and let your head not lack oil.

⁹ Consider life with the wife whom you love all the days of your vaporous life which he gives to you under the sun, all your vaporous days. For that is your portion in life and in your labour at which you labour under the sun. ¹⁰ All that your hand finds to do, do with strength. For there is no work or thought or knowledge or wisdom in Sheol, where you are going.

¹¹ I turned and I saw under the sun that not to the swift is the race, and not to the strong is the battle, and also not to the wise is bread, and also not to the understanding is wealth, and also not to the knowledgeable is favour, but time and chance meet them all. ¹² For also the man does not know his time. As the fish that are seized in an evil net, and as the birds that are seized with the trap, like them the sons of man are caught in an evil time, as that which falls upon them suddenly.

¹³ Also this wisdom I have seen under the sun, and it was great to me: ¹⁴ A little city and few men in it. And came to it a great king and surrounded it and built against it a great siege-work. ¹⁵ And was found in it a poor wise man and he delivered the city by his wisdom. And no one remembered that poor man. ¹⁶ And I myself said, Better is wisdom than might, but to the wisdom of the despised poor man and to his words there was no listening.

¹⁷ The words of the wise in quietness are heard more than the outcry of the ruler over fools.

In chapter 7, Solomon sets out what wisdom (human wisdom) can accomplish, and what it cannot. In chapter 8, Solomon sets out a number of practical uses of human wisdom, concluding again with a reminder to man that he must be humble, because his wisdom is not up to understanding or comprehending the work of God. In chapter 9, Solomon moves on to a number of considerations that follow from what he has set out in the two preceding chapters.

The meaning of verse 1 is a matter of debate among the commentators. The first line is clear. He set his heart to a particular task, to clarify it in his own mind, so that he could make it clear to his readers. The task that he set himself to consider is the state of the righteous before God. What makes the verse difficult is that Solomon follows a pattern that is seen often in Hebrew narrative. That is, a summary statement is made at the beginning of the story before the full story is told. In like fashion here, Solomon has stated his conclusion before he has laid out the full account of what he has considered. The reader must hold off on his reaction until he gets a little further into the chapter before he can fully make sense of what Solomon is saying.

First, however, let us look at his conclusion. He says that the righteous and the wise and their service are in the hand of God. The word 'service' here is translated 'deeds' or 'works' by many of the translations. It occurs only here in the Hebrew Bible. It comes from the root that means 'to serve' and there is a related noun that means 'servant' or 'slave.' So I have taken it here in the sense of 'service,' understanding by that word that Solomon might be intending the service that the righteous and the wise offer to God. Looking at the situation, Solomon concludes that these things are in the hand of God. We do not know from our observation whether these things are acceptable to God or not. That is what Solomon means by 'whether it be love or hatred.' Our own evaluation of the acceptability of our service to God is meaningless. These things must be judged by God, and he alone will determine whether they are acceptable to him or not.

At the very least, men should be aware that the acceptability of their service to God is not based on their own intent in offering it. God himself determines what is acceptable to him in the way of service. We cannot figure that out by observing the world around us. Solomon is implying that we must look to God's revelation to determine what constitutes acceptable service to him.

As he continues into verse 2, Solomon's intentions become more clear. All things alike to all. There is one event (or chance) to the righteous and the wicked. Solomon has already observed that sometimes the wicked appear to get what the righteous deserve, and vice versa. So one cannot determine by observing what happens to someone whether God is pleased with that person or not. This again is a warning against 'karma theology.'

It is possible that Solomon simply means here that all die. It is certainly something that he has said more than once before. But here he simply says 'one event.' Then he begins to list various sorts of people: the righteous and the wicked, the good and the clean, and the one who sacrifices and the one who does not sacrifice. The good and the sinner. The one who swears an oath just as the one who fears to swear an oath. It seems to me that Solomon's point here is not that all alike die, but rather that the same sorts of things happen to all sorts of people. As an example, in our context, all kinds of people get cancer. Righteous people and wicked people. People who are good and people who are bad. People who are ceremonially clean and those who are not. One event has happened to them all. Thus, from simply looking at what happens to a man, we cannot tell whether the attitude of God toward him is love or hate.

In verse 3, Solomon points out that this fact is an evil. That is, one would prefer to know. We, often desperately, want to know not only our own standing with God, but the standing of others as well. Yet God keeps these things hidden. Connected to this, Solomon observes that men are full of evil. This is an allusion to Genesis 6:5 and 8:21. And then men die. Life is full of inconsistencies and injustices. That is vanity. That is proof that the world in which we live is a fallen world. The ultimate proof of a fallen world, for Solomon, is death. And that is the end of every man.

Verse 4 makes the point that as long as a man is alive, there is hope. The contrast that Solomon offers was probably funnier in his day than it is in ours. In Solomon's context, the lion was seen as a regal animal. The dog, on the other hand, was a despised scavenger. So Solomon has flipped the evaluation around. Even a living dog is better than a dead lion. Why so? Because with the living there is yet hope. With the dead, their fate, as it were, has been sealed. The point of verse 5 is that the living, knowing that they will die, have the opportunity to prepare for that death, to use their time of hope to prepare for the time when hope is gone.

The second half of verse 5 considers the dead from the perspective of life under the sun. They no more contribute to this life, and they are eventually forgotten. Again we have here echoes of Ecclesiastes 1:3-11. A generation goes and a generation comes, and the past is forgotten.

Verse 6 continues the idea. When a person dies, all their affections die with them. Furthermore, their share in this life is gone. They no longer have a say in what is done under the sun. Their words may be quoted in an effort to effect decisions made long after they are gone, but they themselves have no part to play, no role in what is done. Solomon pulls no punches here in his depiction of the finality of death as it relates to life in this world. For those dead, there is no hope. For those dead, there is no longer any involvement in the affairs of this life. Those dead are forgotten. Even those closest to the dead, though they miss them and grieve the loss, soon begin to lose them. The faces of the dead become fuzzy to those who are left. Eventually, there is nothing but the vaguest sort of image, and even that is usually more from pictures of the dead than from true memories. The emptiness in the heart of those living remains, but otherwise, the dead are gone and they have no more role to play in this life.

This is grim stuff. It is the reality that Solomon insistently impresses upon his readers. But there is another side to the story. Solomon has recommendations for those still living.

Those recommendations can be summed up in the sentence, 'Enjoy your life as you are able to.' He begins this reflection in verse 7. 'Eat your bread with joy. Drink your wine with a good heart.' Straightforward advice, too rarely taken. For those of us with more than enough, how often do we complain about what we have? As Proverbs 27:7 says, 'One who is full loathes honey, but to one who is hungry everything bitter is sweet.' But God here enjoins us to enjoy the small and ordinary things of life, for he has already approved it. The final clause of the verse, 'for already God is pleased with your works,' is not a general statement that God has already approved whatsoever a man might do. Instead, it is the closing remark on the recommendation that we eat and drink what God has provided in a joyful and thankful manner. This is very much like, 'for this is the will of God in Christ Jesus for you.' 'Investigation proves that life is so constituted that the only satisfaction it yields is the happiness which man is able to experience; that being so, to extract this enjoyment cannot be wrong but must have the approval of the Creator.'[1]

Verse 8 continues the thought. The NLT's 'Wear fine clothes, with a splash of cologne!' is over the top, but reflects the general sense of the verse. 'At all times let your garments be white' is not so much an encouragement to wear *fine* clothes, but rather to wear *clean* ones. Likewise, the use of oil was for improving one's appearance.

Most translations begin verse 9 with 'enjoy.' That strikes me as reading more into the verb than is justified. Literally, it means 'see,' which can have the sense of 'experience.' The idea of enjoyment comes more from the context than from the wording of the verse. The verse continues the commendation of the enjoyment of the ordinary things of life as being the gifts of God. The mention of vanity here is not that life is meaningless. Instead, it is the recognition that life is brief

---

[1] Reichert and Cohen, *The Five Megilloth*, 179.

and we experience the corruption brought by sin throughout the extent of our lives. Yet even in the midst of sin and misery, God has given man good gifts that are to be enjoyed. See life, experience it, with the wife you love. This verse is one of those that leads some to think that Solomon could not have written the book. But such a view fails to take into account Solomon's investigation and reflection on the realities of life. It is indeed possible for someone with a thousand wives and concubines to understand the wisdom and the pleasure of one wife with whom to experience all that this life, vain as it is, has to offer.

'Your vain life' which God has given to you. Technically, 'God' is not in the verse, and the HCSB has taken the third masculine singular verb form as an implied passive, which is possible. However, most translations, rightly, take the implied subject of the verb to be God. That understanding is certainly consistent with the larger context of the book. Life, marriage, work are all appointed by God, and were so even before the fall. The fall corrupted those things, yet even so God gives the gift of enjoying those things. He does not give that enjoyment to all, and he does not give it *always* to those to whom he gives it. Yet when we have the opportunity, we need to enjoy our lives, enjoy our marriages, enjoy our work, as the gifts of God, as the portion he has given us in this life.

Verse 10 is a variation on 'seize the day.' It is a call to diligence and steadiness in our work. To work while it is day, for night is coming when no man can work (John 9:4). Relative to life under the sun, work, planning, knowledge, and wisdom might exist in Sheol, but they have no effect on the present. The reader needs to remember that Solomon is looking at life under the sun, the life that is accessible to our senses. He does not deny life after death, but our senses tell us nothing about the nature of that life. It is therefore necessary to take full advantage of the time we have here, to do what we find to do with our strength.

Following on verse 10, verse 11 reminds us that diligence in our task, though commanded and commended, is no guarantee of success. Solomon's statement here is terse and pointed. Part of the proverbial style is hyperbole. That is, deliberate overstatement to make a point. Solomon is not denying here that the swift sometimes win the race. He is, however, catching us up short, and making us think about the fact that many times, the swift do not win the race. Things do not go the way we expect them to. We make our plans then they don't work out. As Helmuth Von Moltke, said, 'No battle plan survives contact with the enemy.' That is one of the painful realities of life. Anyone who has ever gambled on football (or any other game, for that matter), or anyone who has ever paid any attention to the difference between the predicted outcomes of games and the actual outcomes knows that there is a reason they play the game. The best team doesn't always win. But Solomon has made the point in a much more pithy and terse fashion. Translations such as the CEB and NLT dull the point, and the verse ends up not pricking as it should. Time and chance happen to all.

Verse 12 follows on verse 11 only loosely. Solomon takes the opportunity created by his statement about time and chance to drive home the point that men do not know when they will die. Like animals caught by the hunter, unpleasantly surprised (if we are allowed some anthropomorphism), so men are surprised by their time of death. 'His time' might also be used more widely here, in the sense of being surprised by events. That is, unexpected things happen. We appreciate good unexpected things. Unpleasant and unexpected things, however, are painful. The 'evil' of the net spoken of here is not that the net itself is evil.[2] Instead, the result to the one caught in the net is evil. Likewise, the evil time is the time in which evil occurs to the man. These things are unpredictable.

---

[2] Reichert and Cohen, *The Five Megilloth*, 172.

Solomon is reminding his reader that evil times do come. So we should be as ready for them as we can be. Men must not think that everything will always go well for them. In a fallen world, things rarely work out in an entirely pleasant manner. In one sense, we cannot be ready for these times, because they cannot be predicted. On the other hand we should not, in a sense, be surprised by them, because we know they will come. My impression here is that Solomon is counselling equanimity on the part of people when bad times do come. They serve as a reminder that this is a fallen world, a vain world.

Verses 13-16 give us a vignette similar to the earlier story about the king and his successors in 4:13-16. Some commentators try to connect this to a particular historical event, but that seems unlikely to be the case. That attempt usually occurs when the commentator then uses the event that this supposedly refers to as a way of dating the book. The event depicted here is, however, generic enough that one can easily imagine such a series of events taking place. In 2 Kings 7, for example, the city is saved, at least in part, by four unnamed lepers. No one remembered who those lepers were. Yet they were the ones who brought God's deliverance to the attention of the king and the other city officials. This story is again a commendation of wisdom, but with an unpleasant reminder: the wise man will not be rewarded or remembered as he deserves.

Verses 17-18 provide a transition into the material of chapter 10. In fact, verse 18 probably goes better with what follows than with what precedes. Verse 17 provides a contrast with the end of verse 16. The juxtaposition of the two is similar in nature to that of Proverbs 26:4-5, about dealing with fools. Those verses, contradictory as they appear, are intended to make one point: it takes a real wise man to know how to deal with fools. Some commentators, however (Waltke, for example, in an otherwise very fine commentary), give such a convoluted explanation, trying to remove the paradox, that the two verses end up not making any sense at all. Solomon's point here is that sometimes wisdom is listened to, and sometimes not. Verse 16 might be taken as a warning against the wisdom of the mob, which follows only power, and overwhelms the sensible directions given by the wise. Thus, the folly of the French Revolution overwhelmed whatever good sense there might have been in its beginning. Verse 17 can be taken more in the sense of a recommendation than an observation, or a recommendation in the form of an observation. 'The words of the wise in quietness are heard more than the outcry of the ruler over fools.' I take 'ruler' here more in the sense of 'chief example of' than in the sense of 'king' or 'leader.'

19. Proverbial Wisdom

Ecclesiastes 9:18–10:20

^{18} Better is wisdom than weapons of war and one sinner causes much good to perish.

^{1} Flies of death turn rancid and ferment the oil of the perfumer. A little folly overcomes both wisdom and knowledge.

^{2} The heart of the wise to his right and the heart of the fool to his left.

^{3} And also, according to the way in which a fool walks, his heart lacks and he says to all that he is a fool.

^{4} If the spirit of the ruler rises up against you, do not leave your place, for calmness settles down great sins.

^{5} There is an evil I have seen under the sun: an error that goes out from the presence of the ruler. ^{6} Folly is set in many high places and wealthy sit in a low position. ^{7} I have seen servants upon horses and princes walking as servants upon the ground.

^{8} One digging a pit falls into it, and one breaking down a wall, a snake bites him.

^{9} One setting out stones hurts himself by them. One splitting wood is in danger with them.

^{10} If the iron is dull and the edge of it is not sharpened, then strength he must exert. And the profit of success is wisdom.

^{11} If the serpent bites before it is charmed, there is no profit to the master of the tongue [the charmer].

¹² The words of the mouth of the wise are gracious and the lips of a fool swallow him up.

¹³ The beginning of the words of his mouth is folly and after his mouth is great ignorance.

¹⁴ The fool multiplies words. The man does not know what will be; and what will be after him, who can declare to him?

¹⁵ The labour of the fool exhausts him who does not know to go to the city.

¹⁶ Woe to you, O land, whose king is a youth and your princes eat in the morning.

¹⁷ Blessed are you, O land, whose king is a son of nobles, and your princes eat at the right time—in strength and not in carousing.

¹⁸ In double sloth the rafters cave in and with the idleness of the hands, the house leaks.

¹⁹ For laughter they make bread, and wine rejoices life, and money answers all kinds of things.

²⁰ Even in your thought, the king do not curse. And in the chambers of your bed, do not curse the wealthy, for a bird of the heavens may bring the voice, and the master of the wings will declare a word.

This section is a collection of proverbs intended to consolidate practical wisdom in a number of areas for guiding the reader in his day-to-day life. These verses are connected to one another in much the same way as the verses of Proverbs 10-22 are. That is, key terms connect a verse with what precedes and with what follows, but often with changes in the real subject from one verse to the next.

Chapter 9 verse 18 commends wisdom, but warns against the danger of folly. Here again, the term 'sinner' is more of a wisdom category than a moral category. The contrast between the first and second lines is really that between wisdom and folly, rather than between righteousness and unrighteousness.

It is a truth of which we have all had experience, so needs little explanation.

The sense of 10:1 is very much like that of 9:18, though more picturesque. The translation, however, is a bit more difficult. A painfully literal rendering is, 'Flies of death it makes to stink (and) bubble up (or pour out) oil of the mixer of a precious thing; from wisdom, from honour, a little folly.' The precise meaning of 'flies of death' is disputed, but 'flies characterised by death,' i.e., dead flies is probably the best explanation. 'Mixer of a precious thing' is taken as idiomatic for perfumer, and that may well be right. The idea is that flies that die and fall into the ointment, or that fall into the ointment and die corrupt the ointment, thus ruining the work of the perfumer. This, of course, reflects a time when such operations as the making of perfumes were not carried out in sterile laboratories. The second line, in the terse, cryptic form of the proverb, piggybacking on the first line makes the point that a little folly likewise corrupts wisdom and honour. Examples of the truth of this proverb are too numerous to begin recounting.

Verse 2 reads 'the heart of the wise to his right hand, and the heart of the fool to his left hand.' As we have already noted, in the Old Testament the heart is not so much the seat of emotions, though on rare occasions it has that sense, as it is the seat of the intellect. Thus the proverb is making the point that the wise man is led in the right direction. He understands things properly and in their proper relation. As a result, his thinking does not lead him astray. The fool, on the other hand, (pun noted) does not understand the proper way of things. As a result, he goes wandering off in the wrong direction. Left-handed people should not be offended by the wording of the proverb, though doubtless some oversensitive souls are.

Verse 3: 'And also, according to the way in which a fool walks, his heart lacks and he says to all that he is a fool.' One way of summing this up is that a fool shows himself to be a fool by his behaviour. 'Way' here is not 'manner,' but 'road.' The fool walks on the wrong road. He cannot, or will not, follow directions. Therefore he displays his folly before all.

In verse 4 we again have reflections on how to deal with the king or the ruler. If the spirit of the ruler rises against you, do not leave your place. The idea here is to consider what you should do if the ruler directs his anger at you. The first recommendation is that you do not leave your place. The idea probably is that you should not resign, but rather hold your ground, as the second part of the verse seems to indicate. The key word is 'gentleness' or 'composure,' though it comes from a root meaning 'to heal.' Thus, the proper response to the raised spirit of the ruler is not desertion. That would certainly be understandable in the ancient world, where the displeasure of the ruler could be fatal (consider Pharaoh's treatment of his chief baker (Gen. 40), or Nebuchadnezzar's threat to execute all his advisors if they couldn't explain his dream to him (Dan. 2)). Instead, the wise advisor holds his ground and his composure, and seeks to dissuade the ruler from a rash course of action. Another possibility is that the underling has indeed done something to cause offence to the ruler. In that case, the idea is that a composed, soothing response will allay the anger of the ruler and perhaps, in some sense, minimize the offence.

Verse 5 is the beginning of a related series of proverbs. Solomon begins with the typical introduction of an evil that he has seen under the sun. In this case, the sort of inadvertence (the word 'error' means an unintended mistake) to which one in power is liable. This is not a great evil, but it is something of which Solomon is directing his readers to take note. In a sense, he is saying, if you are ever in a position of power, don't make the following mistake. The word 'ruler' here is not the same as the word in verse 4. It simply means one who has power. It occurs only four times in the OT, three times in Ecclesiastes and once in Genesis 42:6, where it refers to Joseph as the one who was the ruler over the land.

In verses 6 and following, Solomon illustrates the kind of

error that people in power are apt to make. The first example is a fool placed in great heights, which is figurative for a high position. On the other hand, the rich dwell in low places. In the ancient world, though riches were not invariably a sign of wisdom, they were at least a sign of some ability. Thus the person in power should be careful not to appoint fools to office. The previous verses have given some indication of how fools should be identified. In addition, the rich, that is, those with some ability, should not be wasted in positions beneath their ability. Plumptre explains, 'the rich here are those who by birth and station are looked on as the natural rulers of mankind.'[1]

Verse 7 indicates that Solomon has seen that advice ignored, or the person in power has simply made one of those unintentional mistakes. Solomon has seen servants on horses, and princes walking as if they were servants. That is, the proper order of things has been turned upside down. Those who should have been in positions of authority are not, and those who should have been low have been exalted.

The next few verses move away from the proper order of things to a set of considerations about more practical matters. The point of these is that we should exercise care in the daily activities of life. The man who digs a pit should be careful that he not fall into it. The one who breaks through a wall should take care that he not be bitten by a serpent. In the Near East loose rock walls are favourite sorts of places for snakes to hide, so one breaking through such a wall, whether for ordinary purposes, such as breaking it apart to open a space, or for nefarious purposes, such as breaking through to steal, ought to be careful that he not dislodge and anger a snake in the process. In a similar fashion, those who quarry stones or who split wood need to be careful. Again, examples are legion of people who are hurt by the kind of work they do either from poor planning, or careless execution.

[1] Reichert and Cohen, *The Five Megilloth*, 176.

The image in verse 10 has to do with the application of wisdom in planning and forethought. The man who would chop wood (thus the link to the previous verse) with a dull axe will need to put forth more effort. Wisdom tells a man to sharpen the axe first. The sense of the last clause is clear (wisdom is profitable) though the wording is not. That is why the English versions show so much variation. Literally, it reads, 'and profit to give success wisdom.' Obviously, in some sense, any of the English versions is a possible way of translating the line. But in the end, what does it mean? I take it that the idea here is that wisdom gives an advantage in gaining success.

Much of the emphasis in this chapter up to verse 10 has been on the importance of planning as a display of wisdom. In verse 11 the emphasis is on the wisdom of timing. That is, things not only need to be carried out in the proper way with proper planning, they also need to be carried out at the proper time. The snake must be charmed before it bites. Otherwise, there is no point in having the charmer. The right work carried out at the wrong time is ineffective, and likely to be counterproductive.

Verses 8-11 have to do with practical wisdom or common sense. This practical wisdom is profitable, because wisdom guides both planning and execution. It is the fool who rushes into things without planning or without preparation, and at the wrong time. In Numbers 14, the Israelites were zealous to take the land. But it was the wrong time. They had refused the right time. Thus, when they committed themselves to the act, they failed. They acted foolishly, rather than wisely.

Verses 12-15 shift to a direct discussion of the fool, particularly in terms of his speech. Again, the verses here are proverbial in character. They are terse, sometimes to the point of being difficult to comprehend. They require the reader to slow down and ponder what is being said. Verse 12 begins with the wise man and ends with the fool. It contrasts the two in terms of speech. The wise man speaks gracious words. The fool, on the other hand, is destroyed by his own words. Literally, 'the lips of a fool swallow him up.' The image is striking. A fool falls into his own mouth to his destruction. The word translated 'swallow up' is used in the sense of 'destroy.' For example, in Psalm 21:9, 'the Lord will swallow them up.'

Verse 13 shows how bad the state of the fool is, as declared by his speech. His speech is shot through with his folly. He begins in folly, and ends in madness. This should not be surprising to the discerning reader, for he knows that the fear of the Lord is the beginning of wisdom and knowledge. The fool is one who does not fear the Lord. This failure is reflected in his speech. The language here recalls the end of chapter 1. Solomon understands folly. As a result, he also understands how folly affects the speech of the fool. Verse 14, along with a number of passages in Proverbs, as well as the opening verses of chapter 5, make it clear that one way the fool shows himself in speech is in the multitude of his words. Given the conclusion of verse 14, it appears that the multitude of the fool's words are directed at explaining what will happen. But Solomon confronts the fool with the certainty that no man knows what comes next. There is no one, except God, who can tell him what is coming next. And God isn't talking.

According to verses 12-15, fools love talk and hate work. The idea here is not that fools have so much work to do that they are worn out from overwork. Rather, a fool is wearied even by the thought of work. The second line of the verse is clear enough, but its meaning in the context is not. It may be part of a proverb about a fool, that is, he is so stupid he doesn't even know the way to the city. Most versions read it along the lines of the NASB's rendering: 'he does not even know how to go to a city.' But it is possible that the issue is not the way to the city, but rather the going itself, that is, he doesn't have the sense, or perhaps the willingness to go the city, where the jobs are.

Verses 16-17 deal with the fool in the context of the king. The warning is to a land ruled by youths. Youth in itself is not evil (see, for example, the reign of Josiah who became king at the age of eight), but youth generally is unwise. That is why the book of Proverbs is devoted to instructing youth. So a land ruled by youths will generally be a land ruled by the unwise. Likewise, woe to the land whose princes, that is, the royal retinue, eat in the morning. Most translations render it 'feast.' The contrast with the following verse seems to indicate that the problem is not the eating itself, but at both the wrong time (not in due season) and in the wrong way (for drunkenness). That is, woe to a land whose leadership shows itself to be foolish, doing things at the wrong time and in the wrong way. This has been an emphasis throughout the chapter. Wisdom is doing the right thing the right way at the right time (and it takes wisdom to judge those things). Folly may involve doing the right thing, but at the wrong time, or in the wrong way. Often it also involves doing the wrong thing. In contrast, verse 17 views a land where the leadership is born to the role ('the son of nobles'), and where things are done at the right time, in the right way, for the right reason.

It probably requires a brief excursus to deal with. But it should be noted that one of the assumptions of Solomon is that some people are born to leadership roles. Those who are raised in the upper levels of society are more suited to leadership in that society than those who are not. Proverbs 30:22 warns against the servant who becomes king. Though that passage does not expand on it, filling out the idea from other Solomonic passages, there is the fact that a servant, who has been raised in that role, does not understand the ways of power, except from the receiving end of it. Thus, in wielding power, he is unlikely to be able to do it properly or effectively. The result is misrule. Those who have been raised in the courts, as it were, have seen how power is used, both to good effect and to ill. That will not make such a person automatically a better ruler. But he has a better chance of being a good ruler than one who was raised in a servile position.

The point of verse 18 does not seem to be tied particularly closely to either what precedes or what follows. But it may refer allusively to bad rule, which is condemned in verses 16-17. The idea is clear, however. Not being diligent in taking care of things that need to be taken care of results in problems and much worse damage. This certainly is the case with houses. But, moving from the lesser to the greater, how much more is it true with kingdoms. Solomon may well have had in mind the experience of his father with Absalom and Adonijah. In both cases, because David was not careful to deal with these men, they caused greater problems for the kingdom. The heavy-handed character of Solomon's own rule (we can see hints of it in 1 Kings) may have been from his own attempts not to make his father's mistakes.

Verse 19 is something of a conundrum. Some commentators, seeing chapter 10 as a loose collection of proverbs, do not attempt to make any connection of this verse with either what precedes or what follows. However, it may be that the whole of 16-20 is focusing on the problems related to rule.[2] The first clause of verse 19 is literally, 'for laughter they are making bread.' This may allude to the feasting princes of verse 16. That is, mere eating becomes an occasion for overindulgence, for gluttony rather than sobriety. If the country's leadership is thus committed to self-indulgence, according to verse 18, the land will begin to fall into ruin. The second line, 'wine rejoices life' may also fit into the warning against self-indulgent leadership. The last line of the verse has received the most attention, however. Most commentators seem to think that the line is problematic, because money doesn't answer (solve) everything. I think what we have here is failure to communicate. It is a proverbial line. Therefore, it is either hyperbole: money answers most things, or the word 'all' is misunderstood. It could well have the sense that 'all' often does: 'money

---

[2] See the discussion in Reichert and Cohen, *The Five Megilloth*, 179-80.

answers all kinds of things.' This is not only true, it is really indisputable. The real question is the connection of this verse with the context. It may well be that the verse has in view the 'bad' princes of verse 16. The first two lines focus on the self-indulgence of the princes, and the last line should be taken as 'money answers for both,' where the 'all' refers to the food and the drink of the two preceding clauses.[3]

Whatever the case with verse 19, verse 20 certainly brings the reader around to the king again. The primary purpose here is again to remind the reader of the importance of controlling one's tongue. Such self-control is particularly important with regard to those in positions of rule, but the application is far broader.

[3] G. A. Barton, *A Critical and Exegetical Commentary on the Book of Ecclesiastes*, *International Critical Commentary* (New York: Charles Scribner's Sons, 1908) 175.

20. Planning for the Future

Ecclesiastes 11:1-6

¹ Send your bread upon the face of the waters, for in a
multitude of days you will find it.
    ² Give a portion to seven and even to eight, for you do
not know what evil will be upon the earth. Before the
sun and the light and the moon and the stars grow dark,
.and the clouds return after the rain.
    ³ If the clouds are filled, rain will pour upon the earth.
And if a tree falls in the south, or if in the north, the place
where the tree falls, there it will be.
    ⁴ One watching the wind will not sow, and one
watching the clouds will not harvest.
    ⁵ Just as you do not know the way of the wind, or the
bones in the pregnant belly, thus you do not know the
whole of the work that God has done. ⁶ In the morning,
sow your seed, and in the evening, do not let your hand
rest. For you do not know whether this will succeed or
that or if the two of them are good as one.

These verses continue Solomon's practical advice, that is,
the daily usefulness of wisdom. In our day, many dispute the
usefulness of algebra, but no one disputes the usefulness of
wisdom. It must also be remembered that wisdom in the Old
Testament is not a merely intellectual consideration. It has

a moral component as well. The advice here has to do with preparation for the future. The wise man, though he does not know what the future holds, will yet prepare for what may come, as much as he is able. The reader should remember that in those days most people lived day to day. They did not have much in that way of resources to hold on to in preparation for what the next day might bring. But even for those with not much, Solomon's advice rings true.

Verse 1-2 are usually joined together, taken as related advice. The question is, what is Solomon advising? There are two common views, one that tends to be found in the older commentaries, and one that tends to be the more modern view. The older view is that these verses recommend charity or almsgiving. When one is in a position to give charity, it ought not to be withheld. The sending of bread upon the waters means giving to those from whom you have no expectation of return. The finding it after many days is the observation that those acts of charity have a tendency of coming back to the generous soul in other ways. Dividing a portion has to do with spreading around the charity, that as you find those who are in need, provide as you can for them. It is your ignorance of the future that underlies this advice. You don't know how it will turn out. Another way of thinking about this is with regard to the unjust steward in Luke 16. Though he was unjust, yet he was praised for making friends among his master's debtors, so that they might treat him favourably in the future. He did not know if one or another might work for his benefit, so he took steps with many.

The other view, now more common, is that these are essentially economic recommendations. Don't put all your eggs in one basket. The sending forth of bread upon the waters then has in view the idea of not putting all your merchandise in one ship. One bad storm, one shipwreck, and all your goods are gone. Instead, put your goods in many ships. That way one storm or one shipwreck will not bankrupt you. Likewise, dividing among seven or eight has the same idea. Again, the ignorance of the future is the key here. The wise man takes steps to cover various possibilities so that he will not be caught up short.

I don't know that it is either possible or necessary to decide between the two interpretations. Both require the recognition that wise action in the present is necessary. Steps can be taken that might serve to minimize future difficulties. If taking the 'alms' approach, part of what might be in view is the idea that providing for others in the present may put one in a position of being a more sympathetic recipient of aid if subjected to bad times in the future. Admittedly, this is repetitious, but the emphasis is on wise action in the present, because the future can neither be known nor controlled.

Verses 3-6 shift the idea somewhat to a more distinctly agricultural situation. Verse 3 probably has to do with recognizing man's inability to control nature. Things happen. Rain falls. Trees fall. Nothing can be done about either one. One simply has to deal with the consequences. To provide an example: a friend of mine owned a shop that burned down one night. As he talked with one of the firemen at the site, the fireman asked him what he was going to do. His response was something to the effect that he deals with the issues of the day as they come. The previous day, he had run his shop, because that was the issue of the day. This day, he would begin to rebuild his shop, because that was the issue of this day. Wise men cannot control nature, but they can respond with wisdom to those things that happen beyond their control.

Verse 4 makes the point that paying too much attention to things we cannot control can produce paralysis. Such paralysis is the opposite of wisdom. It is folly. We must work while it is light and we can work, not be discouraged from work by a consideration of what might happen. The responsibility of the farmer is to sow and reap at the time of sowing and reaping, rather than to be deterred by the weather.

Verse 5 is a reminder that sums up an idea that has been repeated throughout the book. There is a great deal that even the wisest man does not know about how the world works. The first example given here is the way of the wind. In Solomon's world, those who studied the weather were capable of making general predictions about the weather, but precise predictions were beyond their ability. Lest we think ourselves superior to them, we ought to spend a year comparing weather predictions (especially 10-day and 30-day forecasts) with what actually happens. What we will find is that even with our satellites and computer models, we don't do particularly well over the long run. As an example, the year 2013 was predicted to be a very active Atlantic hurricane season. The actual result was only two named storms, the lightest activity in a generation.

Solomon's second example is the growth of a child in the womb. In Solomon's day, that it took place was undeniable, as it is today. Today, we can film life *in utero*, but the how of it is still a mystery. We can predict the sex of a child, but even those predictions are sometimes wrong. Sometimes doctors are certain that there is something wrong with the child, yet it turns out not to be the case. In other cases, the baby seems to be developing normally, yet at some point something goes wrong. The doctor knows not why. As we cannot understand even these fundamental processes, why do we think that we can understand the work of God?

So Solomon's advice to the wise man is first of all to give up trying to decipher the ways of God. You cannot do it. His wisdom is beyond you. Second, do what your hands find to do at the appropriate time. Be diligent in your work. You do not know the future, so you do not know what will produce the best results. Trust God with the results. That is probably the hardest part. We want to control the future, but we cannot. We must trust it to God.

21. Summary of Life

Ecclesiastes 11:7–12:8

⁷ And sweet is the light and good to the eyes to see the sun.

⁸ For if the years that the man lives are many, let him rejoice in all of them. And let him remember the days of darkness, for they shall be many. All that comes is vapour

⁹ Rejoice, O young man, in your youth, and let your heart be good to you in the days of your prime. And walk about in the ways of your heart and in the sight of your eyes. And know that concerning all of these, God will bring you into judgment.

¹⁰ And put aside vexation from your heart and pass over evil from your flesh, for youth and vigour are a vapour.

12 ¹ And remember your Creator in the days of your prime, before the days of evil come, and the years of which you say, I have no pleasure in them. ² Before the sun and the light and the moon and the stars grow dark, and the clouds return after the rain. ³ In the day in which the keepers of the house tremble; and the man of strength stoops; and the grinders cease because they are few; and those who see become dark in the windows; ⁴ And the doors are closed on the street; and the sound of the mill becomes low; and he rises at the noise of the bird; and are brought low all the daughters of song;

> ⁵ Also from height he fears, and perils in the way; and the almond blooms; and the grasshopper drags itself; and the caperberry becomes useless; when the man goes to his eternal house; and the mourners go about in the street; ⁶ Before the silver cord is snapped; and the golden bowl is shattered; and the bowl is broken at the spring; and is shattered the wheel at the well; ⁷ And the dust returns to the earth as it was; and the spirit returns to God who gave it. ⁸ Most vaporous, said Qohelet. Everything is vapour.

At this point, Solomon begins his final summary. He first surveys the life of a man. He does not use 'vanity' in this passage until he reaches 12:8, but the understanding of the vanity of life runs clear through these verses. He reminds the reader of many of the things that he has already said. First, we are to enjoy the daily aspects of life. We are to enjoy the present, because that is all we have. Light is good, and the sun is pleasant. It is in the small ordinaries of life that we are to find our pleasures, for that is where God has given them to us.

When dark days come we are to remember that they are part of the equation. The future is no more permanent that the past, and the future holds no guarantee that it will be better than the past or the present. We can look forward to the next day, thinking that the next day, or the day after, or surely the day after that, will bring the solution to our difficulties, or the satisfaction that we desire. But to think that way, and to live that way, is to live in a fantasy world. Days of darkness and difficulty are many and are sure to come, so rejoice in the light when it is light, and enjoy the day while it is day. Let the young man rejoice in his youth, not wasting it on an expectation of what might come.

The advice given in verse 9 is commonly misunderstood as an equivalent to today's mantra, 'Follow your heart.' That is not what this verse means. As I have said before, the 'heart' in the Old Testament is not the seat of emotion, but the seat of the intellect, of the understanding. So Solomon's advice is, 'Walk (that is, behave) wisely. Behave with understanding.' And this is the fundamental consideration. God will bring all these things into judgment. That is, the young man needs to understand at the basic, fundamental level, that our lives are lived before the face of God, and that we, truly, and in the end, are answerable directly to him. Therefore, the young man is to put away vexation and evil from his life.[1] Youth is not the time for sowing wild oats, for childhood and youth are quickly gone. They are vanity, and like all time, they must not be wasted in worthless pursuits.

Solomon repeats the idea in 12:1. The young man needs to begin acting in, and living by, faith in his youth. Dark and difficult days are sure to come, and the wise youth is prepared for them. Ahead are years of unpleasantness. This does not mean that there will be multiple years that are unpleasant, but rather that with advancing age and its accoutrements (marriage, children, work) come increasing responsibilities. This verse also begins to look toward the end of life. After all, life is brief. As youth passes quickly into adulthood and adulthood into middle age, so middle age passes quickly into old age. The young cannot appreciate this fact from their own experience, so they need to listen to the advice of their elders and prepare for the days that are sure to come.

Verses 2-7 are a set of images that portray the physical decline of old age. Some commentators try to make this into an allegory, with a specific meaning for each image. Such an approach is reflected in the NLT, which gives what might be called an explanatory paraphrase. The reader is certainly welcome to see that translation, or some of the commentaries that take that specific view of the passage. This approach, however, strikes me as being overly precise. Instead, it appears

---

[1] Suggested by Reichert and Cohen, *The Five Megilloth*, 184.

to me to be primarily an impressionistic set of images. The main point of these images is to lay before the reader the increasing weakness and bodily decrepitude associated with old age. There is, however, another element here that is often not addressed. That is, there is a certain eschatological slant to several of the images. I think the combination is intentional. There are really two *eschatons*, one for the individual and one for the world. The two bear not only a certain relation, but also certain similarities. This is part of the point that Solomon is drawing the reader to. The *eschaton* is approaching, both in the individual and in the world sense. It is incumbent upon each man to be ready for that event. In the following explanation, I'll use death to refer to the personal *eschaton*, and eschatological to refer to the world *eschaton*.

The images in verse 2 strike me as being primarily eschatological. The darkening of the lights of creation, at a secondary level, may refer to the growing dimness of the eyes, as old age advances. However, the contrast with the opening chapter of Genesis strikes me as too obvious too ignore. It is imagery that is also later picked up by the prophets to refer to the world *eschaton*. The return of the clouds after the rain may refer to the inability to stop the advance of age, 'which cannot look forward to a renewal of youth and sunshine, but only to inactivity and final darkness.'[2] But it may also draw in images of the flood. The rain came in judgment of the world, and though there is the promise of God not again to destroy the world by flood, there is yet the certainty of a judgment yet to come.

The images in verse 3 are generally taken to refer to the increasing weakening of the body with advancing age. Precisely which part of the body is referred to in each case is a matter of some debate. 'The keepers of the house' for example, may refer to the shoulders or to the torso. The 'man of strength' are the legs, or perhaps the arms. The 'grinders' are the teeth. And

---

[2] Reichert and Cohen, *The Five Megilloth*, 186.

'those who look' are the eyes. Others take this part of the set of images as drawing on the idea of a manor house in decay. In that case, the 'keepers of the house' are the servants. The 'strong man' is the guard. The 'grinders' are more servants. 'Those that look' out the windows are the ladies of the house that dare not venture out. The reader can readily see how this set of images might also be applied to a village in decay.

In verse 4, the 'doors' are either the ears, or the doors of the house shut against the decay outside, or the village gates shut against attack. 'The sound of the grinding' may also refer to the loss of hearing. Or it may refer to the loss of servants as the manor house undergoes decay. Or it may refer to simply the loss of resources both of grains and workers in a failing village. 'Ris[ing] at the voice of the bird' may refer to the increased agitation of the elderly, with the loss of sleep that often occurs in old age. The image is a little harder to explain in reference either to a village or a manor house. The reference to the 'daughters of song' is also obscure, though it may be related to hearing loss. Or it may refer to the loss of musicians in a manor house when the servants are lost. Musicians would probably be the first to be let go. Likewise, in a shrinking village there would be fewer and fewer musicians.

In verse 5, the first five clauses are generally taken to refer to such weaknesses and fears that attend old age, fears on the street, the white hair of old age signified by the white almond blossom, the limp of the injured aged indicated by the dragging grasshopper, the decline in sexual potency indicated by the use of the caperberry, which was used as an aphrodisiac in the ancient world. The increasing weakness of the human body, and man's inability to control or to change that progression are brought sharply to the fore.

All these things are the case because man goes to his eternal home (literally, the home of his eternity) and the mourners who are left after his demise go about in the streets. It was the custom then, as it is now in the Middle East, to hire professional mourners, so that the dead would be properly mourned. Something similar, perhaps, is found in the accompanying of funeral processions with jazz bands in New Orleans.

The images of verse 6 also signify the approach of death or the *eschaton*, but again in images that are difficult to pin down. The likeness that always comes to my mind when I read this section is a shot from an old Western, where the wind blows the dust and the tumbleweeds across the street of the dilapidated ghost town. Everything is about to collapse. Things are old, worn out, broken, dilapidated. The end has come. As Solomon has insisted throughout the book, this is the end of every man. No man escapes death. In Genesis 5, only of Enoch is it not said, 'and he died.' The statement of verse 7 is a deliberate allusion to Genesis 3:19: 'You are dust and to dust you shall return.' Every man must face God. He is unable to stop the advance of age and the decline of the body that precedes death. These things should help him prepare to meet his Maker, but man so often does not take advantage of that opportunity. Solomon is directing his reader in such a way that those with wisdom will avail themselves of the opportunity to prepare.

Verse 8 returns the book to the point where Solomon began. Again, this is not a hopeless book. This is not a cynical book. This is not an unorthodox, contradictory book. It is a book in which Solomon takes a clear-eyed look at reality. He holds his reader, as it were, by the head, forcing him to look at reality. The reader is thus shown that everything in this life, that is, under the sun, is temporary. It is fleeting. It is a mist that scatters in the wind. That does not make life meaningless. Instead, its purpose is to direct men to faith in God and enjoyment of the joys that God gives in this ephemeral life. The things of this world are passing away. The fool tries to hold on to them. The wise man enjoys them as he is able, but fears God, the Ultimate Permanence. At this point, then, Solomon closes his reflections, leaving only a brief afterward.

22. Afterword

Ecclesiastes 12:9-14

[9] And moreover, Qohelet was wise. Yet he taught the people knowledge. And he weighed the investigation. He straightened many proverbs. [10] Qohelet sought to find delightful words, written what is upright—words of truth.

[11] Wise words are as goads, as nails driven in by masters of collections, given from one shepherd. [12] And for the rest of these my son, be warned. Of the making of many books there is no end, and much study is a weariness of the flesh.

[13] The end of the matter: all has been heard. Fear God, and his commandments keep. For this is the all of man. [14] For every work God will bring into judgment, concerning all that is hidden, whether good or evil.

This afterword is usually assigned to someone other than the author of the rest of the book. Many commentators hold that one author is responsible for 1:12–12:8, and that an editor of some sort has provided the prologue (1:1-11) and the epilogue (12:9-14). Much of the basis of this is the fact that *Qohelet* is spoken of in the third person in both passages. However, to conclude this is to assume that the biblical authors operated on the same sort of assumptions about authorship that we do, a questionable assumption. It is better to assume that the prologue and epilogue have been provided by the author himself, thus serving to place the meditations of the body of the book in their proper context.

Verses 9-10 emphasize the wisdom of the author. This assertion is effectively denied by those who hold that the book is a hodge-podge from a variety of authors. It ties it in to the other wisdom literature of the Old Testament. Perhaps the implication of the first line is that the book of Ecclesiastes is in addition to his other wisdom, which again would fit with Solomon as author. Further, his knowledge was not for himself alone, nor was his wisdom for himself alone. He was a teacher. He taught the people knowledge. Moreover, in order to teach the people knowledge, he weighed, he searched out, he made straight many proverbs. This assertion again reinforces the idea that this book is not a random collection, but rather that it is carefully thought through and evaluated. It is, in that sense, like a modern book that has been written, rewritten, edited and written again in order that the sense and the order of the book might be honed to a fine point.

In verse 10, the evaluation continues. *Qohelet* sought to find 'words of delight' (ESV) or 'acceptable words' (KJV). Though this sort of translation of the phrase is common, it is probably not correct. The word *chephets* is used a number of times in the book. In some cases, it is used in the sense of 'matter' or 'purpose' (3:1). In other cases, such as 5:4, it means pleasure. Perhaps the idea is really that of words that are suitable, words that fit the situation. It gives the reader the image of a writer who has carefully sorted out all his thoughts, who has searched for precisely the right words to express his thinking. Thus, appropriate or fitting words. The rest of the verse continues along the same line: that which is written uprightly, that is, straight words of truth. These verses make the emphatic statement that Solomon has very carefully thought through what he intended to say, and very carefully arranged what he said, and very carefully selected his vocabulary in order to express precisely what he wanted to say. Thus, the idea that this work is a hodge-podge of disconnected thoughts is entirely contrary to the assertion of the author himself. Even if one takes the epilogue to be the product of an editor, the editor's insistence is that this is a well-crafted piece of work.

Verses 11-12 speak of the words themselves and their source. The words are goads. That is, these words are intended to spur the reader as goads are intended to spur the oxen. He also uses the image of nails fastened. That is, they give a solidity to what is said. They, as it were, nail things down. They are planted, nailed down, by masters of collections. They are given by one shepherd. That is, these are the words of God, the one true shepherd. Verse 12 is a final waning to the reader or the student. The idea is perhaps that this book is not intended to be the last word on the subject. Or that Solomon recognizes that it will not be the last word on the subject. These concluding words make the point that careful study is necessary to work these things out, to properly understand them. The problem is that people are often not willing to put in the effort to properly understand these things.

Verses 13-14 bring the main theme of the book out in the conclusion. Everything has been heard. Solomon has laid out his whole argument, his whole case. Now the final consideration is before the reader. Fear God. Again, this is not fear as is commonly thought of. The fear of God in the Old Testament is really the equivalent of faith in the New Testament. This is not the servile fear of an abstract deity that so many find in this book. Rather, it is the knowledgeable faith of the man who has studied his God and knows who he is. The fear of God leads to the keeping of his commandments. 'For this is the whole duty of man' is how the KJV and other versions translate it. But that's not really the sense. It is 'for this is the all of man.' The idea is that this is what makes man whole. This is what fulfils man. It doesn't look like it from our fallen perspective.

But if we have learned the lessons that Solomon has laid before us, then we realize it is this obedience to the commands of God that enables us to live profitably in this ephemeral world. Because, after all, we are answerable to God for everything. We are his creatures, made for his glory.

I conclude with an illustration. I heard the story of a man who began attending church because he and his wife thought that his daughter, who was five or six at the time, needed some religious instruction, and they knew they were not the ones to give it to her. So, instead of merely dropping her off at church, he began to attend with her. Shortly after they began to attend, the preacher began a series on Genesis. The man testifies that when the preacher read Genesis 1:1, 'In the beginning, God created the heavens and the earth,' the hair stood up on the back of his neck, because he knew that it was true, and that he was in big trouble. May that knowledge come to every reader of Ecclesiastes, and may he henceforth live in the true, life-giving fear of God.

About the Publisher

The Banner of Truth Trust originated in 1957 in London. The founders believed that much of the best literature of historic Christianity had been allowed to fall into oblivion and that, under God, its recovery could well lead not only to a strengthening of the church, but to true revival.

Interdenominational in vision, this publishing work is now international, and our lists include a number of contemporary authors, together with classics from the past. The translation of these books into many languages is encouraged.

A monthly magazine, *The Banner of Truth,* is also published and further information about this, and all our other publications, may be found on our website or by contacting either of the offices below.

THE BANNER OF TRUTH TRUST

3 Murrayfield Road
Edinburgh, EH12 6EL
UK

P O Box 621, Carlisle
Pennsylvania 17013
USA

banneroftruth.org